10 Hours Of Guided Meditations For Deep Sleep, Anxiety, Depression & Overthinking:

Positive Affirmations & Meditation Scripts For Relaxation, Insomnia, Self-Love & Energy Healing

Healing Mindfulness & Hypnosis Buddy

© Copyright 2020 My Magic Meditation- All rights reserved.

The content contained within this book may not be reproduced, duplicated or transmitted without direct written permission from the author or the publisher.

Under no circumstances will any blame or legal responsibility be held against the publisher, or author, for any damages, reparation, or monetary loss due to the information contained within this book. Either directly or indirectly.

Legal Notice:

This book is copyright protected. This book is only for personal use. You cannot amend, distribute, sell, use, quote or paraphrase any part, or the content within this book, without the consent of the author or publisher.

Disclaimer Notice:

Please note the information contained within this document is for educational and entertainment purposes only. All effort has been executed to present accurate, up to date, and reliable, complete information. No warranties of any kind are declared or implied. Readers acknowledge that the author is not engaging in the rendering of legal, financial, medical or professional advice. The content within this book has been derived from various sources. Please consult a licensed professional before attempting any techniques outlined in this book.

By reading this document, the reader agrees that under no circumstances is the author responsible for any losses, direct or indirect, which are incurred as a result of the use of the information contained within this document, including, but not limited to, — errors, omissions, or inaccuracies.

Table Of Contents

Introduction 5

Guided Mindfulness Meditation 9

Guided Meditation for Deep Relaxation 22

Guided Meditation for Stress Relief.............................. 36

Guided Meditation for Self-Healing 54

Guided Meditation for Self-Healing While Sleeping 71

Introduction 79

Guided Meditation for Overthinking............................ 82

Guided Meditation for Stopping Overthinking 2 90

Guided Meditation for Overcoming Anxiety................ 95

Guided Meditation for Overcoming Anxiety 2 105

Guided Meditation for Panic Attack Relief 115

Guided Meditation for Overcoming Depression........ 123

Guided Meditation for Overcoming Insomnia 139

Introduction

In the modern world, we are often disconnected from our true selves and the divine power within us. Always busy, in a constant rush, trying to achieve everything and keep up with the world.

We forget about our true nature, about the ability of our magnificent bodies to heal themselves and maintain their perfect balance.

Too often, in our minds, we forget to notice the world around us and to really experience life - true life, here and now. Our minds constantly jump to the past and the future, skipping the present moment. We are so used to it that we don't even notice what's wrong with this picture.

Many of us can't stop our busy minds, and we have no idea that we choose our thoughts. Even worse, many of us are not even aware that we have thoughts that are not the truth.

We are not aware of what's going on within us, but we can see and feel the consequences—our bodies get sick, we feel bad about ourselves, and we suffer from issues on all levels.

So how can meditation help?

The popularity of meditation increases as more people discover the benefits of it. And there are many.

You can use meditation to improve concentration and intellectual abilities, prevent memory loss, increase awareness, reduce stress or anxiety, improve sleep, change ways of thinking, build a positive mindset, and much more.

Meditation can help you calm your mind.

A calm and peaceful mind is where inner peace begins. However, most of us don't know how to turn off our constant stream of thoughts. Meditation helps you learn and practice that. That way, you become the master and your mind becomes a powerful servant that works for your highest good, as it's meant to be.

It helps you de-stress.

Stress is the number-one cause of most health and mental issues these days. There's no more efficient way to learn how to manage it, gain new perspectives on stressful situations, and protect yourself from chronic stress and its harmful effects on the body.

It teaches you mindfulness.

Have you ever wondered how much of life we miss out on while being focused on the past and future? A lot. Being mindful means being truly present and aware of everything—yourself and everything around you. Since the present moment is the only reality we have at any given moment, being consciously present improves your quality of life. Nothing can better teach you to be consciously aware of the present moment than mindfulness meditation.

It helps you gain a deeper understanding and self-compassion.

Meditation is also a way to reconnect with your inner self, your unconscious, and your higher self. Some forms of this practice can help you develop better self-understanding and support you in becoming a better version of yourself.

Meditation helps you recharge, re-energize, and self-heal.

Your body is wise; it's a part of a much bigger intelligence than yours. It knows how to heal itself and bring itself back into balance. You just need to calm your busy mind and move it into self-healing. Self-healing meditation is aimed at helping you learn how to do that, so you enhance your natural healing.

Practicing meditation helps you change your way of thinking and develop a positive mindset.

Thinking positive is a skill, and it can be learned and practiced. Meditation is a perfect way to see our thoughts for what they really are and to realize we have the power to choose which thoughts we want to follow.

Meditation helps you improve your relationships.

It increases patience, tolerance, kindness, understanding, and compassion, which are all key for building, maintaining, and improving connections with others.

There are so many benefits from practicing meditation that we could talk about it for days.

Here, you'll find guided meditations for developing mindfulness, deep relaxation, stress relief, and self-healing.

Remember that there's no wrong way to practice meditation. Just do your best to enjoy the moment.

Guided Mindfulness Meditation

Welcome to guided mindfulness meditation.

Here and now—that's the only reality we really have. All other moments are just in our minds. Being truly present, here and now, means you're living the moment to its fullest. That means being mindful.

Mindfulness means being consciously present in a moment and aware of everything going on within you and around you.

When you choose to consciously live as much as you can, you are choosing to improve your overall quality of life. Practicing mindfulness meditation will help you a great deal to reach that goal.

All you need to do is to follow my guidance that will help you ground yourself in the present moment.

The main goal of this meditation is to wake your awareness of everything going on in your body and in your surroundings. That's why you need to calm your breathing, synchronize it with the rhythm of the universe, quiet your mind, and relax your body. Paying attention to the physical sensations within you will help you calm your mind and step out of your head.

Choose the time of the day when you can be alone and not disturbed. Find a quiet place and make yourself comfortable. It's important to feel the ease in your body so you can quiet your mind. Choose the position that suits you the most—you can either lie on a bed or on the floor, or you can sit on a floor, a chair, or a pillow. Just whatever you prefer and is convenient for you.

Make sure your clothes are comfortable, that all tight pieces of clothing, such as belts, are loosened, and that you are not too warm or too cold. If you want to practice this meditation before going to sleep, get ready for bed beforehand.

I suggest you practice this meditation with your eyes gently open. If you want to close them later during the meditation, that's okay—but try to stay alert.

To begin the meditation, choose one point in front of you and focus your vision on it. Narrow your focus on that point and allow everything else to fade away into the background.

Now, slowly broaden your field of view and allow the background to come into your sight.

Try to notice everything coming into your visual field without turning your head. Look consciously at everything in your sight. Try not to name the things you see, but just be aware of them and their characteristics. This might require some practice and time, but it's worth the effort. For instance, what colors do you see? Don't name them nor judge whether you like them or not. Just notice the colors, the shades, the textures, and the materials of the things in your sight. Notice as many tiny details as you can that you wouldn't have otherwise noticed.

The simplest things in life often turn out to be the best things. Breathing is one of them. It's incredibly simple—an essential life function—yet the most powerful way to ground you in the present.

Bring attention to your breathing. Notice its natural depth (or shallowness) and its rhythm. Just notice for now, without trying to control it. Listen to the sound of your breathing. Now, acknowledge any movements in your body connected to breathing.

Then, intentionally start to deepen your inhale and slow down your exhale.

Breathe in through your nose, counting to four. One, two, three, four.

Breathe out through the nose again, counting to six. One, two, three, four, five, six.

Repeat this breathing cycle a few times. Inhale—one, two, three, four.

Exhale—one, two, three, four, five, six.

Breathe in through your nose, counting to four—one, two, three, four.

Breathe out through the nose again, counting to six—one, two, three, four, five, six.

Breathing like this, with exhales longer than inhales, will relax you and tell your mind everything's okay. You can now rest and relax into the moment.

Take time to breathe consciously, being aware of everything about your breath, and maybe, for the first time, fully experience breathing.

Between every two breaths, there is a small pause. Focus on those still moments, the pauses between every two breaths. Feel the air filling your body and leaving it. Feel it goes into your nostrils and all the way into your lungs, then back outside.

Once again, breathe in—one, two, three, four. And breathe out—one, two, three, four, five, six.

If your regular breathing is shorter or longer than reflected in these numbers, don't worry. Don't force anything; just try to keep your exhales a bit longer than inhales.

There are certainly some thoughts going through your mind. That's perfectly normal and just how our minds work. Being consciously present means noticing them as well as your breathing. Be aware of the thoughts your mind is generating, yet don't engage with the thoughts. Just notice thoughts arise and let them pass by. Imagine your thoughts as colorful balloons flying away. As your breathing slows down, your mind slows down too. There are fewer and fewer balloons for you to release.

As mentioned earlier, pay special attention to pauses between each breath and, now, the similar pauses between your thoughts. Make a link between those two types of pauses in your mind. Allow yourself to be in this gap between every two breaths and every two thoughts. Allow your attention to rest in this space. If your thoughts are still wandering, and you notice that you tend to follow them, just bring your awareness back to your breath and the gap between breaths. Enjoy calm breathing and resting in the pauses.

Now, it is time to expand your awareness of your physical experience.

Invite your attention to your body. There's always so much you can experience on the physical level that you could stay in this moment, yet never grow bored.

Focus on your physical contact with the surface below you. You might experience this contact as warmth or pressure, or the physical border might feel blurred, giving you a feeling you're one with the surface beneath you. Feel your feet on the ground and your back being supported by the chair. If you are in a lying position, notice the surface under your whole body. Feel it supporting your back, your head, and the backs of your legs and arms.

Notice the surface's texture. Is it a flat floor, a soft mattress, a cushy chair, or a fuzzy cushion you're sitting on?

Acknowledge its temperature. Bring your attention to the surface of your body—your skin. Be aware of everything that touches your skin, from the brush of your clothes to the soft texture of your comforter, if you are lying down.

Feel the temperature of the space around you.

Be aware of any smells around you. Focus on each smell for a few moments. Again, try not to name them nor to judge them. Just notice them.

Bring your attention to the sounds around you. There are always many sounds surrounding us and our ears work all the time to process them. We are just used to ignoring most of them. So acknowledge everything you can hear. There might be sounds from outside—voices, traffic, birds, dog barks. Maybe there are sounds from appliances in your house. Or you might hear people in your apartment building.

Listen to the sound of your breathing. Try to hear your heartbeat in your ears. Notice the details in the sounds you are can hear. There are always so many sounds around us, with numerous colors and tones; it's just a matter of whether we choose to ignore them or acknowledge them.

Take a deep breath. Breathe with your belly, so your belly expands on the inhale. Exhale as slowly as you can.

No need to do anything. Allow yourself to simply be. Just be present, in the moment, aware of everything within you and around you. You are a human being, not a human doing. You don't have to do something all the time. It's enough just to exist and be consciously aware right now. Feel the beat of your heart and the flow of your blood within you.

Bring awareness to the aliveness of all parts of your body. Nothing can ground one better than focusing on sensations in the body.

Take a deep breath, expanding your stomach like a balloon.

Breathe out, and focus on your hands. Feel the aliveness in your palms and fingers. Acknowledge all the sensations in these body part. You might feel warmth or tingling in them. If you feel the urge to move your hands or fingers, allow yourself to do it. Feel the movements and be aware of every sensation.

Move your focus to your arms. Notice all the sensations on the surface and within them, from your wrists to your shoulders. Feel the backside of your arms. Notice the temperature of the air around you. By focusing your awareness on a particular body part, you are already relaxing it.

Now bring your awareness to your feet and toes. Feel the tingling in your feet and toes, and how your awareness relaxes them. Allow this relaxed feeling to spread slowly upward to your ankles, your inner legs, knees, and upper legs. Acknowledge sensations in your whole legs—warmth, the brush of your clothes, the touch of the air. Allow your hips, glutes, and pelvic area to relax, and be consciously aware of all sensations in them.

Continue moving your awareness up to your stomach and chest. Be aware of the up-and-down movement of your stomach as it follows the rhythm of your breathing. Feel the air expanding your stomach and chest, and leaving it with your exhale. You might feel bubbles of air in your digestive system or hear sounds from your belly. Notice everything. Then pay undivided attention to the air going in and out of your body.

Breathe in to the count of four—one, two, three, four. Breathe out to the count of six—one, two, three, four, five, six.

Repeat this counting a few more times, focusing on the movement of air in through your nose, to the lungs, to your stomach, then all the way back.

Notice still periods between every two breaths. There's nothing there but pure existing. Feel grounded and allow yourself to relax further, sinking deeper into the surface.

When you notice thoughts running through your head, simpy acknowledge their existence. Imagine these thoughts are colorful balloons, so watch them and let them fly by. Resist the impulse to follow any of them. You might be used to following them, but you don't have to do that. Just stay out of it, observing them. You are not your thoughts. Your thoughts are not reality, nor they have any power over you. Acknowledge what they truly are—products of your mind.

Continue to scan all parts of your body. In doing so, you become aware of each part and your body as an integrated whole.

It's time to bring awareness to your back. Stretch your back and feel the texture of the furniture or floor beneath it. Pay attention to sensations in your back muscles. Scan them by focusing on each muscle, one by one, starting from your lower back. Straighten your spine, and notice the movement of the muscles following that straigthening. As you scan your muscles from the lowest point upwards, feel how they become heavier and softer. Feel the warmth and relief. If there is any tension remaining in your back, send love to that particular point and give it special attention. Visualize the tension melting, releasing all stress.

Now consciously feel your neck. Notice the weight of the head it carries all the time and the relief it feels while you're relaxing. Notice if the muscles of your neck are tensed, and bring focus to them. Bring awareness to your throat. Notice the saliva in your throat and acknowledge the air going through your throat to reach your lungs.

Shift your attention to your head. First focus on the crown of your head. Have you ever be consciously aware of sensations in this part of your head? Relax your scalp, your ears, and your forehead. Be aware of any sensation, movement, and resistance. Feel the touch of hair brushing against your forehead and the temperature on your scalp. Take a deep breath in and visualize you are inhaling pure peace. Allow the air to spread throughout your head, relaxing it, then breathe out. Acknowledge any sensations that might arise within your head.

Focus on your face. Notice all sensations in your facial muscles. Too often, we keep our mouth, cheeks, and other facial muscles tensed all the time without even noticing. Scan your facial muscles with your full awareness. Become aware of any sensation in your eyes and the tiny muscles around your eyes. You can close your eyes if you want.

Take a few deep breaths, visualizing that you are inhaling peace and tranquility. With your exhale, let go of everything that isn't serving your peace of mind and body. Let your exhale take away all the tension in your body and feel your body relaxing as it does. Let your body sink into the surface beneath you, completely supported by it.

Notice the temperature of the air around you. Feel it with your lips, forehead, palms, and lower legs.

Once again, ask yourself what can you hear around you and within you. Try to count all the sounds you can hear. Don't name them or think about them. Just focus on the sounds coming into your ears.

If there is any area of your body that is not relaxed yet, give it special attention. It is trying to tell you something. Sometimes, giving special attention to a tight or unpleasant sensation in our body is enough to make it soften and fade away. Notice the sensation and stay with it for some time, although it might feel unpleasant. If your mind wanders and tries to get busy thinking, gently bring your attention back to the present moment and stay with the experience of the sensation.

Take a deep breath. Exhale slowly. Concentrate only on your breath.

Inhale again. Exhale.

Take a breath again. Slowly exhale through your mouth.

Feel the fresh cool air entering your nostrils and traveling throughout your body. Exhale. Feel the warmth of the air, leaving your body.

Imagine what's going on within your body now – your organs, your muscles, your bones, your nervous system – and watch them all relax. You're giving them time to heal and recharge. Notice your heartbeat and your breathing. Acknowledge the relaxing feeling within the whole body.

Inhale peace. Exhale tension.

Inhale consciousness. Exhale ignorance.

Inhale calmness. Exhale stress.

Inhale clarity. Exhale chaos.

Inhale tranquility. Exhale worries.

Inhale ease. Exhale effort.

Inhale energy. Exhale tiredness.

You are consciously present and aware of this moment, as it is right now. Now you know what it is to be mindful. This moment is the only reality that exists for you. The past and the future are just stories, existing only in your mind. You can feel and experience so much at this very moment. This moment is real, and your thoughts are not. Thoughts are just random creations of your mind. If you still have any thoughts left in your mind, imagine the thought as a balloon you're holding. Open your hand and let it fly away. If you still have stubborn thoughts that refuse to leave you, imagine them as a bunch of balloons you are holding. Now let them all fly into the sky. Whenever you notice that you're following your thoughts and are about to lose conscious presence, bring your attention back to your breathing, surroundings, and the sensations in your body.

When you are completely aware and grounded in the present, you are fully alive. You have your body, mind, and spirit together in one place, and so you become incredibly powerful.

Take another full breath again. Fill your stomach and your chest with peace and calmness. Breathe out as slowly as you can, aware of each moment as you do so.

Now, when you feel ready, you can return to your usual activities. You'll notice that you become more and more mindful and consciously aware of everything you do and everything that goes on in each day of your life.

Guided Meditation for Deep Relaxation

Welcome to the meditation that will help you relax both your body and mind, and achieve a deeper level of serenity and awareness. It's one of the best things you can do for yourself whenever you feel stressed, tensed, or just want to enjoy some deep peace and calmness.

Relaxation is a precious gift we can give ourselves, and its positive effects are tremendous. Most of us go through life tensed, lacking moments of relaxation in our everyday life, not even being aware of the weight we carry around.

We hold stress and tension in our bodies, poisoning ourselves from the inside out. All that accumulated negativity creates energy blocks, which prevents us from fulfilling our true potential and living magnificent lives.

Our bodies and minds need relaxation on a regular basis. So much good is happening when we regularly practice relaxation. By doing so, we open up to the flow of energy and invite prosperity to come into our lives. Practicing relaxing meditation, you'll experience benefits in all fields of life.

Allowing yourself to relax completely is the best thing you can do for yourself and the people around you.

This is time only for you. You deserve it. Relaxation will improve your success in everything you do and the quality of your life in general. So allow yourself to enjoy these moments and being part of the process.

I invite you to follow my guidance.

All you need is some quiet space where you can be alone and not disturbed for a chunk of time. Choose whatever time of day or evening you like. Make sure the temperature of the space around you is pleasant, and use a warm blanket if need be.

Use a few moments in the beginning to find a comfortable position and settle into it. You can either sit or lie down. Take a few breaths, and try to ground yourself in the present moment.

Close your eyes and give yourself permission to take this relaxing journey.

Just listen to my voice, which will gently lull you to a state of deep relaxation. Once you feel completely relaxed, you can easily drift off to sleep, or just enjoy this state, and then slowly get back to your usual activities.

Take a few deep breaths to ground yourself. Breathe in through your nose, into the belly. Hold it for a moment, and then slowly breathe out through your mouth.

Try to exhale as slowly as you can. When your exhales are longer than your inhales, you are sending signals to your brain that you are safe and all is well. Your mind receives the message and, in turn, sends out signals to relax your body. This technique can help you in everyday life whenever you feel the need to calm down and feel grounded. Simple, yet super-efficient. Breathe in through your nose to your belly, then breathe out as slowly as you can. Repeat.

Breathe in. Slowly breathe out through your mouth. Do it again. Feel grounded, feel present, here and now. Allow yourself to relax and enjoy these moments. This is time only for you, this experience is pure joy, and you deserve it.

Now, once your breathing is slower, deeper, and calm, allow it to flow in its natural pattern.

Observe your breathing. Notice the movement of your breath. Feel the air entering your nostrils and traveling through your body, down, into your lungs. Feel it expanding your abdomen, then releasing, going all the way back out through your mouth. Your breath is always with you. You can focus on it at any time and bring yourself into peace.

If you have an expectation about wanting something special to happen during meditation, release that expectation. Don't expect anything to happen, any change to come, or any insights to pop up. Focus only on the present moment and be completely aware of it. This is time reserved for relaxation, along with a complete recharge and restoration of your energy. You don't have to think now. You don't need to be productive or to do anything other than relax now. Give your mind permission to stop and relax now.

If this seems impossible, don't stress yourself about it. Most of us have no idea how to stop our minds and are used to our minds being busy all the time. And that's okay—your mind needs some time to develop this relaxation skill. So don't be concerned if you still have some thoughts going through your brain or some internal chatter. It's not unusual to have inner chatter and other thoughts. What you need to focus on is observing these thoughts and inner chatter instead of engaging with them. Notice, but don't engage. Just let them go. With practice, this will become easier. Notice the thought, and let it go. Random thoughts will still pop up, but they'll fade away into the background once you don't engage. Don't worry; your mind is used to producing numerous thoughts, and, if you are consistent with meditation practice, it will learn with time to relax and rest from thinking.

Now imagine you're walking in the sunshine. It's a beautiful day. Feel the warmth on your skin. The sky is blue and the air is fresh. You're walking up a green hill. The temperature is just right, and you feel as if the air is gently wrapping around your skin. You easily get to the top of the hill. The sight is magical. You can gaze at distant mountains and a dark blue river down in a valley.

Imagine you are lying down on the ground. The sky above you is clear, with just a few feathery clouds in sight. The grass below you is thick and soft, like a comfy mattress. You feel as if you could fall asleep like a baby in the cradle, listening to the birds' singing. Being supported by this grassy pillow, you feel absolutely safe and peaceful.

You can smell the freshness of the air from the hills. It's so pure that you can almost see it shimmering. Take a deep breath, filling your body with sparkling air. Exhale slowly, feeling your whole body relaxing on the soft pillow of grass.

Now, it's time for your body to relax completely, part by part. Bring your attention to your toes. Breathe in, and, as you breathe out, relax your toes, one by one. Relax your feet and let them slightly open up towards the sky. Relax your ankles. Bring your awareness slowly upward to your legs. Feel the grass below your legs. Relax your knees, and then move up to your thigh muscles. Relax those heavy thigh muscles. Feel the texture of the ground on the backs of your legs and glutes. Feel how your muscles become heavier with each breath. Allow your hips to relax and the muscles of your glutes to loosen.

Now, bring awareness to your hands. Our hands do so much for us. They serve us every single day of our lives. They truly deserve rest and relaxation.

Now, place your hands beside your body, with your palms opened to the sky. First, let's relax your fingers, one by one. Breathe in, and, breathing out, relax your fingers. Relax each of your fingers, one by one. Feel the sensations in your fingers; be aware of the tension leaving them. Now, relax your palms and your wrists.

Too often in life, we strongly hold onto things. Usually things that don't serve us. These things might be our thoughts, beliefs, habits, directions, or opinions. These things all come from our ego, and if you truly want to set yourself free, it's time to let them go. Open your hands, relax them, and let off everything you've been holding onto—not just literally, but figuratively, too.

When you let go of everything you've been holding onto, you set yourself free from old, stagnant energy and open up space for wonderful new things to flow into your life. By relaxing and opening your hands, you're welcoming all of that.

Now, relax your forearms, and feel the grass and the ground below them. Bring awareness to your elbows and notice them becoming soft. Release all the tension from the muscles of your arms, and feel them becoming flexible and relaxed.

Now, put the focus on your abdomen, and relax it. Bring your attention to your belly, and notice how it expands with every breath in and empties with each breath out. Your stomach is so relaxed that you can imagine it as a balloon, easily expanding and shrinking in the rhythm of your breathing. There's no effort and no need to control your breathing. Just watch your totally relaxed belly, moving up and down, up and down.

Now, bring awareness to your chest. With each exhale, relax your chest a bit more. Feel your ribcage floating, light yet heavy at the same time.

Now, bring awareness to your back muscles. Relax those muscles, from your lower back to the back of your shoulders.

Starting from your glutes and moving upward, relax all your back muscles, one by one. Imagine your vertebrae in perfect alignment. Visualize your breath going through your spine. Inhale through your spine, and, while exhaling, relax the muscle you're focusing on. With each exhale, your back loosens and relaxes more and more. Feel the press of the ground's surface beneath your back. Notice its structure and temperature. Feel your back muscles become heavy, giving up on any effort, letting the surface support them completely.

The single most important part of this relaxation is relaxing your shoulders. It's time to relax them now. Release your shoulders from your ears, letting them get back into a relaxed position.

The shoulders are where we hold most of our tension, stress, and worries. They carry most of the weight. We are not even aware of this. Letting your shoulders relax is showing yourself that it's truly safe to rest and relax. You are not supposed to be worried and stressed all the time. You deserve to rest. Your shoulders will thank you for this. Let all the weight fall off them and fade away. Enjoy the sense of being free from any weight, worries, anger, and rage. Enjoy being light and free. Your shoulders are recovering and re-energizing now, free from any duty. They don't have to be tensed anymore to carry all the negativity. They don't even need to hold and carry your head—all of that is left to the surface below you now.

You can relax your neck now—both the back of your neck and your throat. Allow your throat to open up and soften.

Your head is resting on the fresh grass, and the grass feels like a fluffy, comfortable pillow. Relax the back of your head. Let your scalp relax, and then your forehead.

Relax your ears. Hear everything that is around you—the soft wind in the grass, birds, and insects around you, the rhythm of your own breathing, and your heart pumping blood throughout your body. Your ears are always on duty, even while you sleep. Allow them to relax now.

Relax your face, including all the tiny muscles that are tensed all the time. Let your cheeks relax. No one is watching, so don't worry about how you look. Let your jaw release, and let your mouth slightly open. Bring awareness to your mouth. Relax your lips, and then your mouth on the inside. Allow your tongue to relax, from its top to its base. Notice how relaxed your cheeks, mouth, your tongue, and your throat are.

Focus on the top of your nose, and visualize how it relaxes, along with your cheeks.

Now, release all the tension from your eyebrows. Relax the forehead, and allow the muscles of your forehand to fall. Focus on the tiny muscles around your eyes, and relax them.

Now, calm your eyes. It might require some time and practice, but do it as best you can. Don't worry if you still can't completely calm and soften your eyes. Allow your eyes to sink into your head. It's incredibly relaxing to calm and rest your eyes. It feels so good.

Focus on the top of your head. Allow your skull to relax.

Now, bring your awareness to the biggest organ in your body - your skin. Your skin is there to cover and protect you, to feel touch and temperature for you, to protect you from the outside world and connect you with it at the same time. Give your skin the rest, relaxation, and restoration it deserves. So, visualize relaxing your skin, from the skin on your toes to the top of your head. Feel the texture of the surface beneath your body. Allow your skin on the back of your body to relax, too.

Imagine your body relaxing on the inside as well. Visualize your internal organs relaxing and resting.

Imagine each organ, then each tiny cell of your body, relaxing and rejuvenating. Every system in your body is releasing all its tension and toxins, repairing itself, and filling with fresh, vital energy.

Now, your whole body is relaxed. Enjoy that feeling of complete relaxation and deep rest.

Focus on your breathing again. Notice its rhythm without trying to control it. It feels so good to be there, completely present and aware, deeply relaxed, and just breathing. Smile to yourself and appreciate this precious moment.

Your body is thanking you now. Mentally say thanks to this moment of deep serenity, to your breath for keeping you alive, to the ground for supporting your body. Feel connected with the surface of the ground and strongly anchored into it.

It's time to let go of everything that's not serving your highest good. Visualize all the weight you've been carrying along with all dark emotions leaving your body and being absorbed by the ground below you. All dark thoughts, all worries, and all doubts—you can name them. Tell them: *I'm letting you go now*, and do it. The ground will receive them. You can repeat this process as many times as you want, with every dark thought, every concern, everything you don't want in your mind and body anymore.

You might notice that your mind is not as calm and relaxed as your body. Don't worry—it's normal to have some thoughts, as it's the mind's job to produce them. Just observe the thoughts, and notice them come and go, come and go. Allow your mind to relax. It doesn't have to grab and follow each thought. This requires some practice, and you'll become better at just observing, not engaging. This is your time for relaxation, not for solving problems, analyzing, or any thinking. Keep your mind out of your thoughts. Just observe them, and let go. By allowing your mind to rest without engaging in your thoughts, you see your thoughts for what they really are. None of them is fact—they are just products of your mind. None of them has any power besides the power you give them.

Now, visualize the blue sky above you. It's a beautiful sunny day. The day is nice, but you notice clouds here and there. Most of them are white and fluffy, but there are also some grayish ones. You already know that those clouds represent your thoughts. Some clouds are light and positive, while others are dark and heavy. As different thoughts pop up in your mind, you see more clouds in the sky. Just watch them float away.

You can feel the freshness of the air and the breeze on your skin. The breeze must be much stronger high in the sky, as you can see clouds are moving much faster now. They all go with the wind and then disappear from your sight.

They fly away, one by one, leaving the sky clear and light blue. You feel peace. Your inner space is exactly like the sky above you. Your mind is calm without the urge to create or follow thoughts. You're enjoying deep inner peace.

It's time to get up. You are standing on the top of the hill, looking at the valley and distant mountains. The fresh breeze has turned into wind. It's pretty cold now, but you enjoy it. You're filling your lungs and belly with fresh mountain air. This wind is not ordinary. It has cleansing power, and it will take away everything you want it to. So it's time to let go everything you don't want anymore.

Take a deep breath, and then with the exhale, let go of any tension that remains. Breathe out any negative thoughts, stress, worries, or fears. Let it all go with the wind—any old, outgrown beliefs, limiting thoughts, or stagnant energy. Let go of all that. Release all hard feelings and bitterness. Let them all go into nothingness.

You can feel the cool wind becoming stronger, and now it blows through your clothes and your body. It blows through your skin, your muscles, and bones, carrying away everything you don't want to hold anymore. You stand in this cleansing wind. Enjoy this unique experience. With each exhale, get rid of all the weight and negativity inside you. Let the pure wind carry away everything that's holding you back. Fill your lungs, your stomach, and both your mental and physical inner space with purity and fresh energy, new thoughts, fresh ideas, and positivity.

With every breath in, name one thing you want to get more of: health, peace, well-being, love, happiness, and so on.

With every breath out, name one thing you want to release: stress, fear, anger, and so on.

Breathe in, and say to yourself what you're filling your inner space with. For instance, you can breathe in, then say "health."

Breathe out, and release all the physical and mental issues you want to get rid of.

Inhale peace, exhale tension.

Inhale wealth. Exhale worries.

Repeat this as many times as you wish, for everything you want to be carried away and everything you want to have more of in your life.

Be one with the cleansing wind; be the active part of this process. When you let go of everything you want, the cleansing is done. You are free from any weight and negativity, and filled with new, vibrant energy.

The wind calms, turning once again into a soft breeze. You feel fresh and energized. Your mind is clean and calm. Your body is entirely relaxed and re-energized. You feel like you are reborn.

You can enjoy this feeling for as long as you want. From this point of complete relaxation, you can drift off to sleep if it's night, or open your eyes, gently move and stretch your body, then get up slowly and move on with your usual activities.

You can come back to this green hill with fresh grass and a cool breeze whenever you want to relax, take a pause from the outside world, and gain new energy.

Guided Meditation for Stress Relief

Welcome to the meditation for stress relief. We are so used to living with constant stress that we don't even notice how it affects our lives. Although a certain amount of stress doesn't do any harm, living with chronic stress is exhausting. It drains our vital energy and causes harm to all our life fields, especially our health.

That's why we need to rest and recover from it regularly. There are many wonderful ways to ease stress and reduce its amount in our lives, such as getting a massage and enjoying a hobby. Meditation is among the most efficient techniques for relieving stress.

Relieve your stress intentionally whenever you feel the need. Doing so will reap miracles for your quality of life.

My voice will be your companion on this journey and will help you calm, relax, and lower your level of stress. You can practice this meditation whenever you feel stressed. Also, feel free to choose particular techniques as applied here to calm yourself before or after stressful events.

Our nature is to be relaxed and in peace. Our bodies and minds have the power to recharge and repair themselves. But as we are stressed all the time, we don't allow them to do so. That's why everyone needs some time to decompress and relax. Don't consider this "me-time" selfish or a waste of time. On the contrary, consider it an investment in your quality of life.

We are taught it's only okay to be busy, productive, and stressed all the time. Give yourself permission to return to your true nature. Allow yourself to spend enough time in peace to process experiences, recharge, and heal yourself.

To begin, find a quiet place and time of day when you can remove yourself from any distractions. Find a comfortable position and follow my guidance.

Stress affects all levels of our being. The most obvious levels are our body, our mind, and our breathing. To relieve stress, we'll focus on those three levels. This meditation will help you calm your mind, relax your body, and deepen your breathing, restoring your lost balance.

Focusing on your breathing first will help you turn your attention inward. Then, we'll relax your body, and, in the end, you'll relax your mind.

When you begin the meditation, you might notice there are many thoughts randomly popping up in your head. Don't stress yourself about them, and don't try to stop them. Just let them pass by.

Just be present, fully aware of this moment and place. Don't expect anything special to happen. Just be open to whatever this experience brings you.

Know that it's okay to have thoughts. It's expected to have thoughts during meditation, and don't stress about it.

Allow yourself to simply be here. Let go of any expectations and inner judgment. Focus on this very moment and be open to whatever it brings you.

Find a comfortable position. You can lie down or sit, but just make sure your back is straight. If you are lying down, your spine should be straight yet relaxed. If you are sitting, also make sure your spine is straight yet relaxed. Once you feel comfortable, close your eyes and take a few deep breaths.

Bring awareness to your breathing.

Pay your undivided attention to your breath—from the moment it enters your nostrils, as it moves all throughout your body, and all the way out. Feel the air in your nose and notice its flow down to your lungs. Feel the air filling your stomach, expanding your abdomen. Then, notice the air leaving your belly and follow it all the way back. Feel the warm air leaving your body through the nose. Be aware of any movement in your body connected with your breathing. Our breathing is magnificent—so simple, yet precious. It keeps us alive even though we hardly ever pay attention to it. Even when it seems like nothing special is happening, there's so much going on in our bodies. Your breath is always with you until the end of your life. You can bring your attention back to it anytime, grounding yourself in the present moment and getting your power back.

Now, try to notice all the sensations breathing provokes in your body. It's time to deepen your breath by counting.

Breathe in, counting to four—one, two, three, four.

Then hold the breath to the count of three—one, two, three.

Breathe out, to the count of six—one, two, three, four, five, six.

Breathe in, counting to four—one, two, three, four.

Then hold the breath to the count of three—one, two, three.

Breathe out, to the count of six—one, two, three, four, five, six.

Let's repeat that once again.

Inhale, counting to four—one, two, three, four.

Hold your breath—one, two, three.

Exhale to the count of six—one, two, three, four, five, six.

Breathe in again, and while you're doing so, visualize that you are gathering all the stress from your body.

Collect all the stress and tension you can, from all your body parts.

Now, visualize you are blowing out a dandelion and breathe out as slowly as you can. With the exhale, let go of all the stress you collected.

Breathing in, visualize you are inhaling calmness and peace. Fill your nose, your lungs, and your stomach with tranquility. Breathe out slowly, mentally saying to yourself: *calm.*

Taking another deep breath, breathe in calmness and peace. Breathe out slowly, saying to yourself: *relax.*

Repeat this series a few times. Enjoy this tranquil, deep, and slow breathing and releasing all the stress.

If any thought comes into your mind (and it certainly will), just notice it and let it go. Bring your focus back to your breath, following its way through the body and the physical sensations it causes.

Mindful and conscious breathing is a practice that greatly reduces stress and helps relaxation. Since your breath is always with you, you can use it whenever you want to.

Stress affects us on so many levels—not only our breathing, but also our minds and bodies. It causes issues with blood pressure, heart, organ function, and even skin appearance. Although our bodies have the ability to heal themselves, they are unable to do so when we are stressed. That's why it's crucial to learn how to decompress and release the stress from your body, and to practice it regularly.

When you manage to calm and relax your body, you are sending signals to your mind that it's safe for it to relax as well.

Now, it's time to relax the body by tensing and loosening it part by part.

To start, bring your awareness to your toes. Breathe in and tense up your feet. Hold the breath while the muscles are still tensed, counting: *three, two, one*. Then exhale and release, relaxing your toes and feet.

Taking the next breath, pay attention to your legs. Tense your lower legs and knees. Still holding them tensed, hold your breath and count: *three, two, one*. And release, letting the muscles relax.

Take another deep breath, tensing your upper legs and hips. Hold the breath, keeping them tensed as tightly as you can, and count: *three, two, one*. And, exhaling, relax the muscles completely.

With the next inhale, tighten your glutes. While holding them tensed, count: *three, two, one*. Then exhale, relaxing the glute muscles.

Breathe in and clench your fists. Hold them clenched to the count of three—*three, two, one*. Breathing out, relax your fingers and hands. Relax your wrists and let your hands open up to the ceiling.

With the next inhale, tighten your arms. Feel the tension in your elbows and upper arms. Hold them tensed to the count of three—*three, two one*. Relax your arms.

Inhale, and tense up your shoulders, lifting them up so that they almost touch your ears. Keeping them lifted, count backward: *three, two, one*. Then slowly exhale, relaxing your shoulders. Allow them to drop down and release all the tension and weight they've been carrying.

Take another breath and tighten your stomach. Contract your abdominal muscles so tightly to pull your navel to your spine. Hold the muscles tensed as tightly as you can while holding your breath. Count: *three, two, one*, and relax. Allow your breathing to return to its natural pattern and your belly to its natural, relaxed position.

With the next breath, fill up your lungs and tense up the muscles of your chest. Hold your breath, counting *three, two, one*. Breathe out and allow your chest to relax. Feel your chest completely relax, as though your ribcage were floating.

Breathe in and tighten the muscles of your lower back. Straighten up your spine, and feel the tension. Hold your breath to the count of three: *three, two, one*. Then breathe out, releasing tension and relaxing the muscles of your lower back.

With the next inhale, tense the muscles in the middle part of your back. Hold them tensed to the count of three: *three, two, one*. Then breathe out, and relax them fully.

Now, feel the tension in your upper back. The upper back is where we hold a lot of pressure and stress. Now, tense the muscles of the upper back and feel all your muscles tighten. Hold your breath, counting: *three, two, one*. Breathe out, and relax all the muscles of the upper back.

Move on to the back of your neck and feel it tensed as you breathe in. Hold your breath—*three, two, one*. Breathe out and relax the muscles of your neck. Feel the relief releasing tension.

Breathe in, visualizing your scalp tightening. Feel the tension in your scalp. Although it's unpleasant, stay with this sensation to the count of three while holding your breath—*three, two, one*. Then breathe out slowly and relax your scalp.

Tense up your forehead. This area is often much too tensed, due to worry or overthinking. You can try to tense it even more by raising your eyebrows. Hold the forehead as tensed as you can, and count: *three, two, one*. Breathe out, and let your forehead relax.

Take a deep breath, and try to tense your eye muscles and squeeze the eyes. Hold them like that—*Three, two, one.* Breathe out, loosening the muscles around your eyes, and allow your eyes to soften and sink into the head. Allow all tension to drift away. It feels so good to calm your eyes.

With the next breath in, clench your jaw. Hold it for a moment: *three, two, one.* Breathe out, and let your jaw drop. Allow your mouth to open up slightly so your teeth aren't touching. Relax your lips. Allow your tongue to drop back, relaxed, and relax the very base of it.

Your whole body is relaxed now. Breathe deeply and mentally scan your body once again. Notice if there's tension anywhere. If you feel some part of your body is still tensed, bring awareness to that part and intentionally relax it as you did above by tensing and relaxing it.

If you notice any tension remaining in any part of your body, visualize that you're setting it free, allowing it to get to the surface. Imagine all the remaining stress collecting on your skin. From here, the stress will float away with your breathing.

Since your mind is relaxed now, your body is getting signals that everything's fine, you are safe, and it's safe for your body to relax fully.

Your breathing is calm, deep, and slow. Your body is deeply relaxed. Now, it's time to relax your mind as well.

The mind is exactly where most of our stress comes from. Our minds are used to being busy all the time. Since they produce tons of thoughts at every moment, our minds are stressed, overwhelmed, and occupied with worries, tasks, scenarios, fears, and all sorts of trash. We are in a constant rush, so we don't leave enough time for our minds to decompress, slow down, and recharge. That is the main cause of many, many problems. For instance, most of our health-related come from the inability of our minds to rest and heal. That's why it's crucial to learn how to soothe and relax your mind. Every part of our body needs some time to rest and repair, even dedicated workers like our brains.

If you notice that your mind is full of all sorts of thoughts running in all directions, don't be upset by that. Your mind is used to doing that, and you can't just turn it off as if you're pressing a button.

Instead, take a deep breath.

When the next thought arises in your mind, just notice it. Resist the urge to follow it. You don't have to engage in each thought that pops up in your head. Just notice it and, with your exhale, let it go. Repeat the same with the next thought. And the next thought.

As you do this, you'll notice your thoughts slow down. The rhythm of your breathing becomes the one that sets the pace.

It can also help if you imagine your thoughts as balloons. When your thoughts are balloons, they float to you. You catch them gently for a moment and then let go, watching them float away. Some of them will float to you quickly, some of them float to you more slowly. Eventually, you'll do the same with all of them, letting them go and watching them fly away.

As you go on with this practice—breathing, noticing, and letting go—you'll notice that your thoughts became slower and lighter. They will look lighter, like soap bubbles or feathers. Notice the feather floating to you. Just blow it away and watch it pass by.

For every dark, hard thought that bothers you and causes you stress, visualize a small, dark cloud in the sky. Depending on how stressful or hard a thought is, give it a proper dark shade, from light gray to black.

Repeat this for all of the thoughts that stress you out. Once you've mentally placed all of them in the sky, it's time to let them go. Watch your imagined dark clouds. Take a deep breath, and, breathing out, release the dark clouds.

Once you are done with sending your stress to the sky, it's time for relief. Watch your stressful thought and the dark cloud you created for it. Breathe in, and, as you breathe out, imagine you are releasing all the stress. While doing so, watch how all the darkness is leaving the cloud. Its color turns lighter and lighter until it is entirely white and fluffy.

Repeat this with the next thought and cloud. Breathe in, gathering all the stress and darkness. Breathe out, let go, and watch the cloud become snow-white.

With the next in-breath, take up all the darkness from the next cloud and release it all with your out-breath.

Repeat this practice for a while. Repeat it with every stressful thought and dark cloud until all of the clouds become snow-white, light, and feathery. There's nothing hard or dark in your mind anymore.

Feel how light and at ease you are. Feel free from any stressful thoughts, and enjoy this feeling.

Once more, take a deep breath, and, as you exhale, visualize yourself blowing the first white cloud away. It flows away pretty fast, as if there's a strong wind in the sky, and disappears in the distance. In the place where it used to be, there's clear blue sky now. Again, breathe in deeply, and, as you breathe out, blow the next cloud away.

Do this for as long as you need to clear all the clouds from the sky.

Now, the sky above you is clear and light blue—the same as your mind. It's calm, light, and clear. You feel ease and serenity. Your mind is deeply relaxed now.

Now, with your body deeply relaxed and your mind completely calm, pull your attention back to your breathing. You don't need to control your breathing, or count it. Just observe your natural, calm, and deep breathing. Breathe in through your nose and breathe out through your mouth, mentally saying these affirmations to yourself as you do so:

Take a deep breath. *I am relaxed.* Breathe out.

Breathe in. *I am calm.* Breathe out.

Breathe in. *I am at ease.* Breathe out.

Breathe in. *I am tranquil.* Breathe out.

Breathe in. *I am wonderful.* Breathe out.

Breathe in. *I am at peace with everything outside and within me.* Breathe out.

Breathe in. *I feel all the cells of my body are relaxed now.* Breathe out.

Breathe in. *I am confident.* Breathe out.

Breathe in. *I am skilled.* Breathe out.

Breathe in. *I am focused.* Breathe out.

Breathe in. *I can handle anything that life brings me.* Breathe out.

Breathe in. *There is peace within me.* Breathe out.

Breathe in. *I am relaxed.* Breathe out.

Breathe in. *I am intelligent.* Breathe out.

Breathe in. *I am calm.* Breathe out.

Breathe in. *I bring light and ease with me wherever I go.* Breathe out.

Breathe in *I am powerful.* Breathe out.

Breathe in. *I can handle everything with ease.* Breathe out.

Breathe in. *I am in harmony.* Breathe out.

Continue repeating the following affirmations as you breathe in and out.

I am calm.

I am relaxed.

I am at ease.

I am tranquil.

I am confident.

I am skilled.

I am focused.

I can handle anything that life brings me.

There is peace within me.

I am intelligent.

I am calm.

I am wonderful.

I am at peace with everything outside and within me.

I feel all the cells of my body are relaxed now.

I bring light and ease with me wherever I go.

I am powerful.

I can handle everything with ease.

I am in harmony.

I am at peace, completely relaxed now.

Your body is now relaxed from the top of your head to your toes.

Bring awareness to the contact of your body with the surface beneath you. Visualize the surface as an incredibly comfortable cloud. It's exactly the same size as your body, and it's here to support you and cradle your relaxed body. This cloud is the comfiest place you've ever reclined on. Enjoy resting on it.

The cloud slowly moves higher, taking you off the ground. You are relaxed, knowing you're safe. So you're resting completely on the cloud that takes you up to the sky.

You're looking at the ground. From here, everything looks tiny, as if it's all made from Legos. You can see colorful land, cities, woods, fields, mountains, rivers, and oceans.

Now, try to locate all those things that used to stress you out. You can't even find them, so tiny they are. Can you even imagine how insignificant they are? All those worries and concerns that used to bother you, they're smaller than a speck of dust. You can't even see them from your safe, fluffy cloud. Here, you feel no stress or worries on your personal relaxing cloud—only calmness, serenity, and deep relaxation.

Suddenly, you notice your cloud begins to shine with golden light. The light becomes brighter, and you realize it's shining from the center of the cloud. It looks as if the sun is shining through the cloud, as if it's at the center of the cloud. With each moment, the light becomes stronger, and the whole cloud shines brightly now. You can feel the pleasant warmth as the light enters your body and spreads through it. You look at your feet and notice they glow, and now your legs are shining with this golden light. The light is moving upwards through your body, reaching your stomach and chest. Your hands and arms are now glowing. Now your head is radiating the light. Your whole body shines. You can also feel the light spreading inside you on the inside, bathing your internal organs, filling your heart and your blood.

The light has cleansing, relaxing, and healing powers. It's the remedy for any type of stress. You are full of shimmering golden light, and you radiate it all around you, spreading peace and calmness. This deep peace is far bigger than yourself; it's everywhere, within and around you. It wraps and covers you like a cozy blanket, comforting and further relaxing your mind and body, thoughts, emotions, and every cell in your body.

If there's still any dark and stress remaining anywhere within you, it's been dissolved now by the divine golden light.

Enjoy the experience of bathing in the healing golden light. Stress is just a distant memory now. You don't have to experience it ever again. Instead, you can come back to this deep peace whenever you want. Whenever you feel stressed, you can rest and relax on your cloud and bathe in golden light.

You are absolutely relaxed now. All the stress has left you. Your body is completely relaxed, your mind is calm and clear, and your breathing is deep and slow. You are at ease.

Your cloud gently lands on the ground.

You slowly move your hands, then your legs. You gently stretch your body and open your eyes. When you are ready, you get up from your cloud.

You are relaxed and re-energized now, free from stress. From here, you can drift off to sleep or get back to your daily activities.

Guided Meditation for Self-Healing

Welcome to the guided meditation for self-healing. Every one of us has the ability to heal ourselves. Sometimes we just need to be reminded of this power. This meditation is aimed at helping you awaken your abilities to heal yourself.

Whether you have a severe diagnosis or other health issue, or you just don't feel very well, this meditation will help you. You'll gain benefits from it immediately after finishing it. Regular practice of this meditation can ease even serious conditions and make severe illness disappear.

You might not be completely aware of this power within you—a power that can help you heal the worst conditions. That power is the same as the divine power that created you.

Our natural state is balance. Our bodies have the ability to repair themselves and to keep themselves in harmony. Problems with health are often consequences of being out of balance for a while and not being aligned with the divine power within us. The good news is that this process works in the opposite direction as well. So if you succeed in restoring the lost balance back, your health will immediately improve.

But your body and mind need some peace and quiet time to heal and repair. If you are always busy and active—in a constant rush, often stressed, never completely relaxed—your body has no time to recharge and repair itself. That's why meditation is the perfect way to enhance your self-healing power. Your body is naturally wise, and it knows how to work magnificent things without your engagement. All you need to do to help it is to move it out of the way and allow your body to open to what's the best for it. Your busy mind is the main obstacle in this natural process of self-healing. It needs to be calmed so your body can regenerate.

The main goal of this meditation is to remind your body how to heal itself, and to calm your mind.

Throughout this meditation, you will learn how to relax your whole body, calm your mind, slow and deepen your breathing, show appreciation and love to your body, and remind your body of its natural self-healing powers.

You can practice this meditation at any time. For the best results, however, I recommend you do it regularly. It is most efficient to practice it as a part of your evening or morning routine.

Whatever time you choose, make sure you won't be disturbed for about an hour. Dedicate this time to yourself and your healing, and make this time a priority. Pause all distractions, and turn off notifications and ringers.

Lie down and find the comfiest position for yourself. If it's more convenient, you can also sit. However, I recommend you do this meditation lying down and using earphones for the best experience.

To empower your body to use its self-healing abilities, you must achieve a state of deep relaxation first. To reach that state, pay attention to my voice and follow my guidance.

First, make sure you're comfortable and pleasantly warm. Straighten your back and straighten your legs, spreading your legs slightly apart from each other. Straighten your hands beside the body. Before we begin, ground yourself with a few deep breaths.

Intentionally slow your breathing. Make sure your exhales are longer than your inhales. That way, you're sending signals to your mind that everything is OK and it's safe for you to relax.

Take a breath through your nose to the count of four—one, two, three, four. Breathe out through your mouth to the count of eight—one, two, three, four, five, six, seven, eight.

Repeat it. Breathe in, counting one, two, three, four. Breathe out ,counting one, two, three, four, five, six, seven, eight.

Do it once again. Inhale—one, two, three, four.

Exhale—one, two, three, four, five, six, seven, eight.

If your breathing can't reach these numbers, don't worry. Do your best, especially focusing on the long exhales.

The main thing now is being gentle with yourself. So don't force yourself in any way; there's no such thing as being unsuccessful in meditation.

Allow your breathing to return to its natural pattern.

With every inhale, visualize the air you breathe is white, healing light. With each exhale, let go of negativity. Everything that doesn't serve your good—it's time to let it all go. Holding onto negative experiences and bitter emotions are like toxins, slowly killing you from the inside out. Let them go.

Inhale white, healing light.

Exhale tension.

Inhale light. Exhale anxiety.

Inhale light. Exhale anger.

Inhale healing. Exhale hatred.

Inhale light. Exhale resentment.

Inhale healing. Exhale pain.

Do this for a while until you feel yourself let go of all negativity you've been holding inside.

Now, it is time to relax your body. This is crucial, because only from this completely relaxed state can you really talk to your body, send it love and gratitude, appreciate it, and encourage it to activate its healing power. Only when you are physically relaxed and have managed to calm your mind, your body can repair itself.

Breathing slowly and consciously, bring your attention to your toes and feet. Tense your feet, from your toes to your heels, then count to three—three, two, one. After you've counted, allow them to loosen. Enjoy the relief. Relax all the way up to your ankles. Then intentionally tense up the muscles of your lower legs. Hold them tensed for a moment, counting to three—three, two, one, and release. Relax your knees.

Now, bring awareness to your thighs. Feel the front and the back of your thighs. Tense the heavy thigh muscles. Count three, two, one, then allow them to relax. Allow your legs to open up to the ceiling, completely relaxed. Squeeze your glutes as tightly as you can. Hold them tensed for a moment—three, two, one, and relax them. Allow your glutes, hips, and pelvic area to relax.

Take a breath in and dedicate breathing out to even more of your lower body, relaxing it. Repeat this a few times. Feel the ease spreading throughout your lower body, making it so heavy that it sinks deeper into the surface beneath it.

Make sure your hands are lying straight down beside your body, with your palms up. Notice the sensations in your fingers. Stretch and tense them for a moment, and then let them relax. Relax your palms, hands, and wrists. It feels so good to rest your hands. They do so much work for you.

Now, move your attention up to your forearms. Tense them to the count of three, two, one, and then release them. Relax your elbows. Move up to your upper arms. Tense the muscles and hold them tight for a moment. Count three, two, one, then allow them to loosen. Your entire hands and arms are relaxed, from your fingertips to your shoulders.

Now, notice how your stomach as it goes up and down to match the rhythm of your breathing. Intentionally squeeze all your abdominal muscles and pull your navel to your spine. Hold them tensed for three, two, one, then relax, allowing your belly to get back to its natural, relaxed state.

Take a nice, deep breath and fill your chest to the full capacity, so your chest muscles are tensed. Three, two, one, then breathe out, allowing the muscles to loosen. Notice how relaxed your stomach and chest are.

Now, bring your awareness to your back and feel the surface below it, supporting it. Tense up your back muscles from the lower back to the upper back. Breathe in and hold them tight, and with your out-breath, relax your lower back. Inhale deeply again, and as you exhale, relax the middle part of your back. Move your attention to your upper back, breathe in, and with your next exhale, relax your upper back. Feel how loosened and relaxed your back is, as if you've just gotten a massage. Allow your back to sink further down into the surface beneath it. Feel how light you are, as if you are floating yet being strongly supported.

It's time to relax your shoulders now. Breathing in, tense them up as much as you can, so they're almost touching your ears. Then, with your exhale, allow them to drop and relax. Feel the muscles of your shoulders loosen, becoming elastic and soft. Continue to breathe in, and relax them more with each exhale. When you relax your shoulders, notice how your whole body relaxes. Feel the relief. It feels so good to shake off all the burdens from your shoulders and finally give them much-deserved rest.

Now, breathing in, gently push your jaw to your chest to tense up your neck. Breathing out, bring your head back and allow your neck to relax. Bring full awareness to your throat as you breathe in again. With your next exhale, allow your throat to soften and open.

Breathing in, clench your jaw once more. Breathing out, release it, allowing it to drop.

Breathing in, tense up your facial muscles by squeezing them, group by group, and then relaxing them as you breathe out. Relax your lips, your cheeks, your eye muscles. Relax your mouth and your tongue.

Inhaling, tense up your scalp and your forehead by raising your eyebrows. Exhaling, let them relax. Relax the back of your head and the top of your head. Feel its weight on the surface below you, and enjoy the sensation of being cradled by the surface.

Your whole body is now completely relaxed. Feel the ease and tranquility. Breathe deeply and slowly, and enjoy these moments of deep relaxation. Your organs, systems, blood, bones, and cells are all relaxing now. They are all regenerating and healing. There's so much happening in your body right now. Appreciate these moments of deep, re-energizing rest.

How often do you take time to appreciate your body and its incredible abilities? How often do you tell it how grateful you are for having it, and for everything it does for you? It is time to tell your body how grateful you are for it, and how much you love and appreciate it.

To start, mentally thank your feet and legs for holding you up and taking you everywhere you want to go. It's such a blessing to be able to change your location by simply moving your feet.

Now, thank your glutes for supporting you while you are sitting. Mentally say "thank you" to your genitals for bringing you joy, and your reproductive organs for giving you the possibility to reproduce. Thank your urinary and digestive systems for cleaning out your body and getting rid of everything you no longer need. Moving upward, thank your stomach for digesting food for you, without any conscious effort from you, enabling you to use nutrients. Now, thank your lungs for keeping you alive by making you breathe and use oxygen. Thank your back for the support it gives you, holding you up. Thank your hands for doing so much for you—holding, bringing, taking, carrying, hugging, creating, and so much more. Thank your neck for holding up and moving your head.

Too often, we are not aware of how blessed we are to just be able to move, to breathe, to walk, to see. Acknowledge all your blessings. Feel how grateful you are from the bottom of your heart.

Your mind is a magnificent thing. It delegates all the functions in your body, manages all the activities, and rules your thinking, far better and faster than any machine. Thank your brain for doing such a spectacular job.

Thank your mouth for enabling you to express yourself, to communicate, to taste the food you eat, to kiss. Say "thank you "to your nose and eyes. It's a precious gift to be able to see. You can see colors, faces, nature. You can see the faces of people you love. Isn't that alone enough for you to be grateful for the rest of your life?

Your body needs to hear that gratitude and appreciate from you. So allow appreciation to overflow you. If you truly allow yourself to feel deep gratitude for all of your blessings, you may even experience tears of happiness.

There's no better medicine in the world than love. Love has the power to heal everything. Nothing will help your body recover more than when you show it how loved it is. Make your love and appreciation for it a regular practice using this meditation. Mentally pour love into every part of your body.

Begin from your feet again. Mentally tell them, "I love you," and focus on really feeling it. Moving up, send lots of love to your legs, your hips, your glutes. Now feel the love for your belly and chest. Your back also needs to hear, "I love you." Pour love into your hands and arms. Say "I love you" to your shoulders and neck. Then, fill your head with pure love. Mentally tell your whole body, "I love you. You are great. You do amazing things. I pour love into every part of you. Love helps you heal, and I want you to be healthy and happy." Pour love into every organ, muscle, and bone. Pour so much love into each cell as it can hold, so every cell of your body becomes a tiny star that spreads the love around it. Send so much love to your heart that your blood becomes pure love. Everything in your body is now bathing in love. Your body is full of love. Your organs work cheerfully—your heart pumps love, and the blood flows joyfully in this cheerful rhythm. You self-love is curing everything. It repairs, rejuvenates, and heals everything that needs to be fixed.

If there is some part of your body that needs special attention, pour extra love into that place. Infinite and unconditional love is spreading from your heart.

You are the one who heals yourself and does it by using the most powerful cure: endless love.

Now you are deeply relaxed. Your breathing is slow and deep. Your body is full of divine, infinite, healing love. Now, you can talk to your body and it can hear you, and you can empower the process of self-healing whenever you want.

Remind your body of its natural power to heal itself and restore balance. Tell it that you trust it and its natural wisdom.

Now, it's time to tell your body everything you want. Listen to these statements and repeat them, either mentally or out loud.

Body, I love you.

I pour love into you.

You are perfect, just the way you are.

You deserve to be perfectly healthy.

Health is your inborn right.

You are meant to be balanced and work as a whole.

You can heal yourself, and you know exactly how to do that.

You are wise.

I trust you.

I allow you to do whatever it takes to heal.

You don't need help—just my trust and support, and I am giving both to you now.

I allow divine power to guide me and to restore you to your natural state of harmony.

I listen to you, I understand you, and I appreciate what you have to tell me. I know you do that because you need my attention.

I let go of everything that stands in the way to my healing.

I'm ready to let go of any negative emotions, limiting beliefs, and holding onto anything toxic.

You know the way, and I trust you.

I believe I can heal myself. I can heal every cell and every organ within me.

I love you. You are amazing and deserve to be completely healthy and happy.

I know you have everything you need for healing, and you will heal perfectly, in the way that is best for you.

Now, visualize a massive golden gate in front of you. You push it gently and it opens, revealing a beautiful garden. You step into the garden. There's so much green—trees, flowers, and grass. The silence in the garden seems magical. You can hear only birds in the trees and insects in the grass.

The sunlight is shining through the shade of the trees. As you step down the path, you can hear the soft trickling sound of water. There still no water in sight, but you can hear it. You go further down the path in the direction of that gentle sound.

This garden is large. Finally, a marble pergola arises in front of you, and you discover that's where the sound is coming from. Coming closer, you can see a pool there. The water is sparkling and crystal-clear. You know that this water is healing water, which helps the body to remind itself of its self-healing power.

You sit on the side of the pool, putting your feet in the water. To your surprise, your feet start shining. You decide to get fully into the water. The water is only waist-deep at this side of the pool. You look down at your legs, and you can see they are glimmering. You feel as though the water is massaging your feet, legs, and hips. With each step forward, the water goes a bit deeper. You are moving on, enjoying the feeling, and knowing that healing in your body is happening right now. Finally, you dive in and feel the water wrapping you like a luscious warm blanket. The water shimmers above your head, and your whole body is now sparkling with its glimmering shine.

Getting out of the water, you feel renewed and refreshed, as if the water washed away everything you needed to shake off.

Your body is now reminded of its powers and abilities to heal. It's full of energy and strength. You know that the healing process is underway within you.

Beside the pergola, you notice an outdoor daybed with a canopy. You know it's here for you. So you lie down on the daybed and make yourself comfortable. You can feel a soft breeze on your skin and the comfort of the mattress. You can hear the water trickle and smell the fresh grass.

Your whole body is now relaxed, rejuvenated, and full of fresh energy. You breathe deeply, knowing that a new part of the healing process is about to begin.

Take a deep breath in and imagine a healing, golden light entering your feet. As you breathe out, notice how your feet are shining brightly.

Breathe in again and feel the light enter the muscles and bones of your lower legs. Breathe out, and visualize your legs shining with golden light. Breathe in the light to your upper legs, allowing it to fill your thighs and hips. Your hips and whole legs are aglow with golden light. On your next inhale, fill the light entering your pelvic area, and on your exhale, see the bright light radiating from your glutes and pelvis. Breathing in, see the healing light fill your stomach. Breathing out, see the bright light spreading up from your center.

Now, inhale the healing light and feel it fill your chest. Exhale, and see your chest shine.

Breathe in the golden light through your spine and allow it to spread all over your back. Feel the golden light enter every muscle of your back. Breathe out, and see how your back glows with the light. It seems as if you are lying on a star.

Breathing in, imagine the light entering your fingers and spreading through your hands. The golden light is filling your lower and upper arms. Breathing out, notice your arms and hands shining gold.

The golden light now moves up to your shoulders, and they begin to shine. With your next breath in, your neck and head are now filling with the healing, golden light. Exhaling, notice how your head is shining brightly.

The light now moves through your skin, wraps around your organs, penetrates all bones and muscle tissues. It moves through your cells, and they bathe in the golden, healing light.

While your body is healing in the golden light, using divine wisdom and its natural powers to heal, you can empower it by sending love, blessings, and supportive thoughts. To build perfect health and achieve balance, you need to adopt new thinking patterns. To do that, repeat these affirmations below mentally or out loud. These affirmations will become your new beliefs and help you create a supportive environment for healing.

I have the power to heal.

I am strong and powerful.

My body and mind are healing now.

I deserve to be perfectly healthy. That is my natural right.

I am ready to forgive and let go.

Life is supporting me.

The Universe has my back.

I love myself unconditionally.

I choose health.

I am full of energy.

All my cells are healthy and vibrant.

I am grateful for my body and its wisdom.

I am thankful for my positive, healthy thoughts.

I am grateful for the perfect balance of my body and mind.

I am complete.

I am whole.

I feel great and am full of energy.

I allow my body and mind to heal.

I love life, and life loves me back. It has a lot to give me, and I am ready to experience it.

I am in perfect harmony and at peace with the world. I allow divine energy and higher intelligence to guide my body and heal it.

Take a nice, deep breath. Breathe out slowly.

When you're ready, gently open your eyes. You can move on with your daily activities, feeling fresh and re-energized. Or, if you want, let yourself drift off to sleep and have nice dreams.

Guided Meditation for Self-Healing While Sleeping

Welcome to the meditation for self-healing. Whether you're not feeling well, have a diagnosis, or if you suffer from chronic pain, this meditation will help you harness the ability of your body to heal itself. During this meditation, you'll be talked into a relaxed state. From that state, you can talk to your body, send love to it, and empower it to heal.

This meditation is aimed to empower the self-healing abilities of your body while you are asleep. If you fall asleep during the meditation, your subconscious mind will listen to my words and help your body in its self-healing.

To begin, prepare for bed as usual. Find a comfy position in bed, and let this meditation lull you to sleep while your body recovers and re-energizes itself.

Slowly calm yourself before this healing journey begins. Let's do a short breathing exercise. Breathe through your nose, counting to six—one, two, three, four, five, six. Then, exhale through your mouth to the count of ten—one, two, three, four, five, six, seven, eight, nine, ten. If you can't reach those numbers as you breathe, don't be concerned in any way. Do what is convenient for you.

Repeat this sequence for a short while. And then, let yourself flow into your natural breathing pattern. While inhaling, imagine you are breathing in a beautiful, glittering light. While exhaling, imagine you are threating out all worries and negativity. Feel how your body grows more and more relaxed with each exhale.

Imagine you are lying in a beautiful, green garden full of colorful flowers. You're listening to insects in the grass, the birds in the trees, and wind whistling above you. Feel the peace and serenity of this garden.

Now, we'll relax the whole body. Breathe slowly and deeply. First, concentrate on your feet. Relax your feet. Relax your toes, heels, and all of your feet. Then relax your ankles and lower legs. Feel the entire length of your legs relaxing, from your knees to your thighs. Bring your focus to your thighs—both the front and the back of your thighs. Feel how your thighs relax more and more with each exhale. Your toes, heels, and feet are now deeply relaxed. Your ankles, lower legs, knees, and thighs are now deeply relaxed.

Focus your attention on your hips, glutes, and pelvic area. Relax your glutes and observe how, with every breath, your glutes and hips become more relaxed. And, with them, the whole lower half of your body also relaxes.

Bring your awareness to your hands. Relax your fingers and palms. Relax your wrists. Relax your forearms, then your elbows and upper arms. Your palms and fingers—relaxed. Your wrists—relaxed. Your forearms, elbows, and upper arms—all of them are relaxed.

Bring your attention to your stomach and chest. Observe how easily they move in the rhythm of your breathing. Relax your chest completely. Relax your stomach completely. Focus on your lower back, and relax your lower back. Feel the surface under your back, and relax your back, part by part, from your lower back and then slowly moving up to your shoulders.

Feel the peace within you and around you. Feel how your body is giving you thanks for this moment. There is so much good happening right now!

Now, relax your shoulders. The most crucial part of whole-body relaxation is the shoulders. Relax them and let them loosen. Observe how they relax more and more with every exhale. Notice how, by relaxing the shoulders, you loosen your whole body. Feel the relief.

Relax your neck. Relax the top of your head. Relax your forehead. Relax your ears. Relax your cheeks. Relax your lips, and let your jaw hang loose. Soften your eyes. Relax your eye muscles completely.

Breathe deeply and feel the peace. Your body is fully relaxed now.

Now, imagine a small white cloud above you. It's a beautiful cloud, and it's here only for you. It brings you healing. The cloud is right above your head. Are you excited? Do you feel happy about what the cloud brings you?

It's beginning to rain from the cloud. It's a rain of light. Feel the drops on your face. It's a healing rain. You can imagine it as you want—whether it's a light, small crystals, or pure water. Connect it with healing.

Your whole head is shining now in healing light. Enjoy it. You know what's going on now. The cloud moves down, above your neck. The raindrops fall over your neck. It starts shining too. Now, both your head and the neck shine.

The cloud moves down, and it's now above your shoulders, chest, and stomach. Feel the soft, warm rain of light. Feel the healing. Watch yourself glowing—your head, neck, shoulders, chest, and stomach.

The cloud expands above your arms. Your arms and hands begin to shine. The cloud grows more, and now it's above your hips, pelvis, glutes, and genitals. These parts are now shining in the healing light. Your head, neck, shoulders, chest, stomach, arms, legs, hips, and glutes are all shining in the healing rain.

The cloud moves down, and healing raindrops are falling over your legs. Observe how your legs begin to glow. Do you feel the rain? Can you feel how it serves you and its healing purpose?

The white healing cloud is now above your whole body, and it's the same size as your whole body. It rains over your body, and all your body parts are shining. It's a rain of light, rain of health, and you shine brightly.

Say thanks to this moment. Feel grateful for the healing that's happening in you right now. If you have any health challenges, you can now bring your little white cloud above the part that needs healing. If you don't have any particular health issue, let the rain fall all over your body. Visualize yourself shining brighter as you heal.

If you have brought the healing cloud above a particular part of your body, imagine that part glowing. As it shines, it begins to work perfectly. All the cells of your body are happy to restore the balance that your body needs and deserves.

Right now, you are giving an incredible gift to your body. Your body is thankful, and it is going to show you appreciation. Enjoy this feeling of healing going on inside you right now.

Any tension that remains in the body now releases itself in the light's comfort, as the light continues to spread through every cell and every atom. As the healing light rains all over your body, your skin may tingle or feel warm. You feel all the stress and pain draining away under the drops of light.

The soft rain of light is enveloping you and spreading out—warm and powerful.

Enjoy the relaxation and feeling that the rain is bringing you. Rest in it, allowing it to do its work of healing you.

You are filled with pure, loving energy. See the healing light radiating from the center of your body.

From this relaxed state, while your body is healing itself using the rain's infinite wisdom, you can send yourself loving thoughts to support the healing process. It's time to release the old negative thinking patterns that have caused disease and disruption in your body, and to adopt new thinking patterns. It's time to build perfect, vibrant health.

Listen to my voice as I repeat the positive statements below. Allow these ideas to enter your subconscious and help you build positive new patterns that create health in your body and mind.

You can repeat my words mentally or just listen to these affirmations and let them become your new beliefs.

I am healing my body and mind.

I am one with life.

Perfect health is my birthright.

I forgive all those I need to forgive.

I forgive myself.

I feel growing love for myself.

I take care of myself because I love myself.

I am choosing health for my body, mind, and spirit.

I am grateful for my amazing body and all the wonderful things it does every day.

I am grateful for my healthy body and my healthy mind.

I am calm and strong.

I am completely healthy.

All the cells of my body are healthy and vibrant.

I am full of positive energy.

I am full of life.

I am loved. I am enough. I am complete.

I am always healing, and I feel good.

I am letting go of everything that doesn't serve my highest good.

I am letting go of fear. I am letting go of anger, blame, sorrow, guilt, jealousy, blame, and tension.

I am at peace. There's no need to struggle.

I am a wonderful expression of life.

I have the power within me, and it's the same power that has created me. Now, I allow that power to heal my body and mind.

The past has no power over me. I'm letting go of it now.

I am unique and magnificent.

I am worthy of love just because I exist.

I accept and appreciate myself.

I'm willing to heal. I deserve all the best life has to give me. I deserve to be perfectly healthy.

I am in perfect balance and harmony with the world. I allow divine energy to circulate throughout my body and help it use its higher intelligence to heal.

Take a nice, deep breath and exhale, visualizing the flowers and grass around you.

Sleep well, and have sweet dreams, knowing your body is healing. Good night!

Introduction

We live in a frantic world, often in a rush, neglecting our true nature and our souls' needs. This fact can easily make us flip out of balance. In turn, our minds cannot calm down, constantly jumping to the past or future, entirely overlooking the present. So we spend too much time in our heads, too little time in reality. We then experience different issues, such as anxiety, panic attacks, depression, or poor sleep.

Fortunately, there is an incredibly simple, natural, yet highly effective solution for all these issues. Meditation gains more and more popularity these days as people discover its many benefits.

It's almost unbelievable how much a simple practice like meditation can transform one's life, help with so many issues, and restore one back to balance.

However, meditation is not a replacement for conventional medical help. If you suffer from any mental issues, please use meditation and enjoy all its benefits, but also be sure to seek professional medical help.

So how can meditation help with overthinking?

Our minds are genuinely devoted workers, which is great—except when it's not. If you've ever had a situation where your mind goes into overdrive and you can't stop excessive thinking, you probably understand what I mean.

We're supposed to be masters of our minds, not their servants. But if you can't find the on/off button of your mind, you can't be its master, right? Luckily, meditation can tremendously help you become your mind's master.

Practicing meditation helps you learn to calm your mind, choose your thoughts, and finally regain control of your thinking. You'll learn how to use all the magnificent tools you already have, like your focus, imagination, and awareness. You won't let your mind drive you wherever it wants, chewing its old trash over and over again. Instead, you'll become the one who chooses and decides how to use the mind's powers.

How can meditation help with anxiety, depression, and mental health?

Anxiety is often a consequence of our mind being too much focused on the future, trying to solve all possible problems and scenarios before they happen. Most of our mind's fears will never come true, but meanwhile, we miss out on the present.

Not to mention how awful we feel. Our mind's fears turn on all the panic buttons in our body, putting us in fight or flight mode. If you try to solve the problem on a rational level by thinking even more about the problem, you're getting yourself in an endless spiral. Rather, the solution is on the other side—by stopping useless thinking, and focusing on physical sensations and conscious presence. Meditation is the answer.

The same goes for when you experience panic attacks. If you're having an acute anxiety or panic attack, it might be hard to remind yourself that you are not in real danger. But meditation can help you calm your body and breathing, which sends signals to your mind to calm down, thereby bringing you relief.

Meditation can also help with overcoming depression. If you suffer from depression, it will help you look at things from different perspectives and gain new insights.

Meditation is a wonderful way to reconnect with your inner self, along with rediscovering your true nature and the incredible power within you. Meditation will help you tremendously in coping with any issue and improve your overall quality of life.

The guided meditations that follow have been created to help you on this journey. Just listen to my voice, relax, enjoy the moment, and allow the process to unfold.

Guided Meditation for Overthinking

Welcome to the guided meditation for overthinking.

Please, listen to this meditation only when you can safely bring your full awareness to your complete comfort and relaxation.

This guided meditation session is aimed at helping you finally release yourself from overthinking and create peace in your inner space. It will also help you learn to calm your mind by training it to observe more and engage less.

This meditation is designed to help you free yourself from constant, useless mental activity—that is, the tendency of your mind to be busy all the time. This practice will help you gain significant insights into the thinking patterns that don't serve you, so you can end them and experience the positive benefits of letting them go.

You've probably noticed that at times, your thoughts can build up so much that you simply can't stop them anymore. They become a constant mental chatter that causes you stress and anxiety. Our minds are used to being busy all the time with unhelpful mental activity. Your mind might have developed habits of worrying, overanalyzing, and reliving personal events over and over again. Your mind needs problems to solve, so it seeks problems no matter if they exist or not. You might feel trapped or locked in an endless spiral of thinking without the ability to stop. These thinking patterns are frequently connected to chronic anxiety and depression.

Fortunately, there is an exit from this thinking spiral and you can find relief from it. The solution isn't to think more, but the opposite: to step out of your head. Focusing on physical sensation and learning to be truly present in here and now will help you stop your unwanted thinking. Practicing mindfulness meditation will teach you how to do that.

With these simple techniques that comprise this meditation, you'll learn how to train your conscious mind to focus on more productive matters, switch from useless mental activity to enjoying present-moment sensations, be consciously present, and change your emotional responses.

Let us begin.

Choose a time in the day when you can focus solely on relaxation and won't be disturbed for a while. Find a comfortable place where you can be alone, listen, and enjoy inner silence.

Find a comfortable position and posture. You can either sit or lie down, but just be sure that nothing is drawing your attention. Your back should be straight and all your muscles in an effortlessly relaxed position.

Once you find the best posture for you, bring your attention inward. Focus on your breathing. Don't try to control or hold your breath; just observe it and be aware of each breath.

Notice everything you can about your breath. Notice the cool air entering your nostrils and going down, through your airways, to your lungs and stomach. Notice your stomach and chest rise and fall in the rhythm of your breathing. Become aware of all the muscles engaging that help your chest and stomach rise and fall. Become aware of your ribs expanding and contracting with each breath. Feel the air coming all the way back to your nose and out. No need to control your breath or change anything; just breathe in your natural rhythm and observe, letting go of the need to control.

Now, become aware of the temperature of your body. Notice any warmth and coolness. Some parts of your body might be warmer than others, and some parts of your body may be cooler than others. That's normal for all resting bodies.

Acknowledge any sensations of warmth or coolness in your hands and fingers. Notice the warmth or coolness in your feet and toes. Notice any sensations of warmth or coolness in your legs and arms. Notice any sensations of warmth or coolness in the center of your body.

Just become aware of these sensations and acknowledge that they're perfectly normal. Accept them and allow yourself to stay with them for a moment.

As your body relaxes, you might notice some movements. Acknowledge those movements without forcing your body to be totally still. Become aware of all the movements of the body. Notice that some parts may feel more relaxed than others, while others may feel tension or tightness. And that's alright. You don't have to force any relaxation. For now, it's enough to acknowledge those sensations. Just allow your mind to observe and accept everything for what it is. You don't have to do a thing. You don't have to think or control anything.

Allow yourself to be at your normal pace. You don't have to rush anywhere. You are at the right place, at the right time. You don't need to be anywhere else. This is time just for you, for your relaxation and for gaining a better self-understanding.

Meditation will help you learn about yourself and get to know yourself better. You'll better understand your reactions, behaviors, and you'll grow the ability just to observe and accept things for what they are. You will learn to be fully aware and present in every moment.

As you continue to breathe consciously, you are fully present in the here and now.

If you want, you can slow your breathing now. Allow your next in-breath to be just a little slower and your next out-breath to be just a little longer.

By slowing your cycles of breathing, you're sending signals to your mind to slow down. As your mind receives that feedback, your body and mind alike continue to gently slow.

It feels so good to calm your mind. Notice you don't have any excessive thoughts. You are not using much thinking energy. You are simply thinking in a normal manner and naturally asking your body to slow down and calm its breathing.

Notice your slow breathing. It's so easy and effortless. As you bring your focus to your breathing, you feel deeply relaxed and fully present.

As you observe each breath with a clear space in your mind, you notice every thought that arises. Just observe each thought that your mind wishes to create. These thoughts might be internal judgments, evaluations, labels, phrases, words, or images—any kind of distractions. Sometimes your thought may be a description.

Your mind is not used to being quiet. It has a need to do something, or at least, to describe or name things. Just note whatever it is that your mind wants to create. Become aware of the temporary nature of thinking.

Thoughts come and thoughts go.

You always have a choice: to follow your thoughts, or let them go. Instead of following your thoughts, choose to remain a little further removed from them. By doing so, you are allowing yourself to stay outside of your mind's evaluations and judgments. Instead, you allow yourself to simply be, by simply noticing these creations of the mind.

So allow any thought that arises to just exist there. There is no need to try to control thinking. There's no need to try to change thoughts or thinking. Simply acknowledge the thoughts, allow them to be there for a while, and give them space to play.

When you give up trying to control your thoughts, acceptance and allowance will make such thoughts come and go whenever they want, and the thoughts will eventually fade away.

Yes, those thoughts are yours. But you also know and understand that who you are is much more than just your thoughts.

You witness the sparks of thoughts come and go, almost like shooting stars across a clear night sky. As a single thought comes into your mind, you easily notice how it carries its own certain energy. Some thoughts have particularly strong energy and call for attention. Others are quieter.

But you can always stay outside all your thoughts by observing, resting, and relaxing.

From a comfortable distance, you can witness and watch as each thought arises and simply passes. As you are calm and observant in each moment, you can choose to turn your focus and awareness inwards back to your breathing—breathing in and breathing out. You are always able to return to this focus on your breath.

Now, allow your awareness to note and observe small sensations that come with each breath. In this way, you are training your observant mind. So notice the cool air as it enters your nostrils, passes through your nose, and becomes slightly warmer as it moves down through your airways. Feel it enter your lungs.

There's no need to hold your breath. Just remain mindful and observe your natural breathing cycles, allowing your body to breathe deeply and completely in its natural rhythm. Don't try to control your breathing. Just silently observe each breath.

This technique is known as mindful breath awareness, and it is a powerful technique. By allowing yourself to focus on breathing in this simple way, you can gently guide and return your conscious awareness back to your breath.

And as you allow individual thoughts to enter your awareness—wherever or whenever they arise—you offer them your calmest acknowledgement. You allow them to pass by, and their energy fades, burns out, or disappears. You let thoughts pass by, offering no resistance.

By using this technique, you can observe who you really are. You are so much more than your thoughts. You're observing, and calmly detaching yourself. By calming yourself, you always remain in the present moment.

You are gaining the understanding that you are more than your thinking and your reactions. There's always one more part of you that is always observing, watching, and witnessing. You are easily able to return to your breath as often as you need. You can always make a choice to remain present in the moment by coming back to your breath, breathing in and breathing out.

You are consciously present now. Your mind is peaceful now.

You can remain in this mindful state for as long as you wish.

If you wish, you can drift off to sleep from here. Or you may choose to remain awake and alert, calmly observing your breathing for as long as you want.

When you are ready, slowly open your eyes, get up, and go on with your usual activities, aware that you can always come back to this state of complete mindfulness.

Guided Meditation for Stopping Overthinking 2

Welcome to the guided meditation that will help you stop excessive thinking. Feel free to use this meditation whenever you feel the need to reach a state of peace without excessive thoughts. This meditation will have you find mental calm.

Make yourself comfortable in a sitting or lying position. For a better experience, I recommend that you listen to this meditation with earphones.

Breathe deeply, focusing particularly on your exhales.

Bring awareness to your breathing. Feel more relaxed with each exhale. Breathe deeply in and out, using your stomach.

Bring attention to your feet. Relax your feet.

Relax your toes, heels, and your whole feet.

Relax your ankles. Feel the relaxed sensation in your ankles.

Focus on your lower legs and intentionally relax them. Relax the front and the backside of your lower legs. Completely relax every part of your legs.

Continue to breathe deeply, focusing on your out-breaths.

Relax your knees. Relax your thighs, both the front and the backside of your thighs.

Notice that your toes, heels, and feet are relaxed. Your ankles—relaxed. Your lower legs, knees, and upper legs—relaxed.

Bring awareness to your glutes and your hips. Relax every part of them. Feel the whole lower half of the body relax. With every exhale, your glutes relax further.

Now, concentrate on your palms and hands. Relax your hands. Let your fingers relax. Relax your wrists.

Continue to breathe deeply, concentrating on your exhales.

Relax your arms, allowing your elbows to loosen. Relax your upper arms. Your fingers, palms, wrists, whole hands—relax all of them. Your lower arms, elbows, and upper arms—relax all of them.

Now, bring awareness to your stomach and chest. Breathing deeply, relax your stomach and chest.

Now, concentrate on your lower back. Feel all the muscles of your lower back. Relax your lower back and let this relaxed sensation move upwards to your shoulders.

Allow your shoulders to relax and feel the relief. With each out-breath, your shoulders relax even. Even when you think you have relaxed them completely, you can still relax them a bit more.

Observe how your whole body is more relaxed as you continue to relax your shoulders.

Now, let your neck relax. Relax the back of your head. Allow your cheeks and forehead to relax. Relax your ears.

Relax your mouth and jaw, letting your jaw fall loose. Relax and soften your eyes. Relax all those tiny eye muscles.

As you relax, notice your thoughts. It's normal to have thoughts. It's natural. Don't resist them and don't try to fight them. Just acknowledge them and choose which of them you want to engage.

The main purpose of this meditation is to create your safe place, your peaceful room, where you can enter whenever you want to rest and calm your mind.

Imagine your mind as a house with rooms in it. You have separate rooms for work, for family, for health, for relationships, for finances, and for love. You have a room for each segment of your life.

Also, imagine you have rooms for your worries and problems. Now, enter one of those rooms. You find that it's loud, full of thoughts and worries. As you stand in that room, observe which thoughts are in there. Observe them, listen to them. As you do, you notice one thing: those are not your thoughts. These thoughts belong to the room that you have entered. How do you feel while watching and listening to the thoughts in this room? Which emotions do they provoke? Do you feel worried, stressed, or frightened?

Now, exit that room and go to your room. This room is pure white. It's a room without thoughts. You see yourself entering that room—white, bright, clean, and airy. Open the door and enter the peaceful space. There's nothing else. It's absolutely quiet there.

Observe your body now.

Observe the peace you feel in that white room. This room is your safe place from now on.

Stay in the room for a while, absolutely conscious. You are aware that this room is the room without any thoughts. Acknowledge the peace and silence in this room. There's nothing but pure existence here.

Peace. Calm. Serenity.

Now, once more, intentionally enter one of the other rooms that are full of thoughts. Choose the worst room, the one with the loudest worries, the most negative thoughts, and the problems that bother you most.

As you stand in that room, observe those thoughts. Watch them.

Now, you feel differently because you know now you can exit this room whenever you want.

Once more, go again to your safe room—the white and quiet room. Once you open that door, feel the silence and peace. There are no thoughts here, just absolute peace.

Now, you know there are many rooms in your mind. But there's always one safe room where you can enter, rest, and be at peace. Go to this room whenever you feel you want to rest from your thoughts. If sometimes you find yourself in loud, negative thinking, don't fight it or blame yourself, just be aware you have entered a room full of thoughts. So remind yourself that you can always exit that loud, unpleasant room and go to your safe and peaceful room.

Now, stay in your safe room. Look around. For the first time, you realize that you can actually see the peace and hear the silence in this room. Acknowledge that this is a space without thoughts. You have the power to choose to be there—in this room—whenever you want.

Guided Meditation for Overcoming Anxiety

Welcome to the guided meditation for releasing anxiety. It is aimed at helping you calm your mind and find relief from excess worries and chronic stress.

Suffering from anxiety can be overwhelming at times. This meditation will help you reduce it and eventually set yourself free from it.

Before you start the meditation, choose a time of the day when you know you won't be disturbed for about half an hour and find a silent place where you can be alone.

Take time to make yourself comfortable, lying on your back, if possible, with your hands relaxed next to the body and legs straight, relaxed, and slightly opened.

Once you find a comfortable posture, I invite you to listen to my guidance. This meditation session will teach you how to find relief and find a place of inner peace whenever you need it.

This is the time to rest your mind and body from anxiety. You are safe now, and you can observe your anxiety from a safe distance. It's safe to relax now, and it's safe to look from this place at all the thoughts that provoke your anxiety.

Now, let your body and mind relax. Allow yourself to release all the tension and disturbing thoughts, and experience a sense of deep peace.

Now, give your thoughts permission to rest. You don't need them right now. This is the time for rest from thinking or doing anything else. There's nothing to be worried about. You are safe now, in a place of complete serenity.

Most often, anxiety occurs because we are too much in our heads and too little in the physical world. Also, we are constantly focusing on the future and the things that might happen. Most of those things never happen, except in our heads. The only reality that exists for us is this moment, here and now. And if you pay attention, you'll notice that at this moment, all is well. So this meditation practice will help you learn how to ground yourself and become truly present in this moment.

It's safe to pause, rest, and relax now. Things have their natural rhythm, and all will be well. You'll be fine, and the anxiety will pass. You won't feel tension forever. You just need to learn how to let it go.

Know that you're in the right place, doing the right thing. There's no need to be anywhere else. There is nothing else you should be doing right now.

Your natural state of being is calm and relaxed. There's nothing wrong with you if you have trouble reaching this natural state – you just need to remind yourself to get back into balance. The key is never to think more. You can't find relief by producing more mental activity. The solution is to calm your mind and be present.

Now, bring your undivided attention to this moment. Don't try to solve anything in your mind. Just let your thoughts pass by.

Bring attention to your body. Notice how it feels. Notice if you feel particular tension in some parts. Focus on each body part and notice exactly how it feels. Doing this, you're already making the first step towards relief and stepping out of your head.

Anxiety is undoubtedly unpleasant. But it's not dangerous as it seems. You are safe. You are stronger than what's bothering you. You are more than your thoughts and stronger than your fears.

Keep your attention on your body. Scan your body, devoting undivided attention to each part and relaxing it.

Notice the most tensed areas of your body, where you are holding the most stress and anxiety. Give some extra love and attention to those parts, trying to relax them as much as possible. Breathe deeply, and with every exhale, try to relax those parts a bit more.

Start focusing on your toes. Focus on them and intentionally relax them. Now, relax your whole feet. Let your ankles relax. Allow this relaxed feeling to move upwards to your legs. Let your knees relax. Loosen your thighs. Allow your hips and glutes to relax. Notice the entire lower half of the body relaxing more and more.

Notice if there's still any tension remaining somewhere in your lower body. If there's any part still holding the anxiety, remember it. You'll come back to those parts later.

Now, invite your attention to your stomach and chest. Notice how relaxed your stomach and chest are as they rise and fall with your breathing. Allow your chest muscles to relax. Feel how your ribcage is floating.

Feel the press of the surface beneath your back. Imagine you are breathing in through your spine. Then, start to relax your back muscles from the lowest point upward, part by part. With each exhale, relax your back muscles a bit more.

Once you reach your shoulders, take a deep breath and exhale, now relaxing your whole back.

If you notice some parts of your back are still tensed, make a mental note.

Now, focus on your fingers. Allow all of them to relax. Allow your palms to relax, and notice how your hands open up toward the ceiling. Relax every part of your hands. Then allow that relaxed sensation to move up to your arms.

Now, we come to a crucial part of relaxation—your shoulders. Your shoulders are where we hold and carry most of our anxiety, worries, stress, and fears. Most often, our shoulders are constantly tensed while we are not even aware of that tension.

So focus on your shoulders. Feel all the tension and weight you've been carrying in them. If you are used to keeping your shoulders tensed all the time, it might be difficult to relax them. Just be patient and do your best. Breathe in. Breathe out, allowing your shoulders to drop down. Do it again--breathe in, then breathe out through your mouth, allowing all the tension and anxiety to fall from your shoulders. Let go of all the weight, all the worries, stress, and anxiety. Breathe in. Breathe out, and relax your shoulders a bit more. Even when you think your shoulders are completely relaxed, there's still space to relax them more. Breathe in. Breathe out, and allow your shoulders to relax even more. Notice how nice it feels to relax your shoulders. It's like getting a relaxing massage. Notice how your whole body relaxes even more as you relax your shoulders.

Now, let your neck relax. Allow your throat to open up and relax, and the back of your neck to soften.

Notice if there's any part of your neck still tensed, and make a note if so.

Make a conscious effort to relax your ears and the back of your head. Feel the weight of your head on the surface below. Relax your facial muscles. Relax your mouth. Allow the jaw to relax and drop down. Relax your tongue. Don't worry about how you look right now. Relax your cheeks. There's no need for any tension in your face. Our faces are often tensed all day long as we play our social roles.

Relax all of your face now. Allow your forehead and eyebrows to relax. Relax all those tiny muscles around your eyes. Calm your eyes and allow them to relax in your head. Notice how good it feels to calm your eyes. Relax the top of your head.

Take a nice, deep breath, and with your exhale, relax your whole body once again.

Once again, scan the whole body with your complete awareness. Notice all those parts that still hold anxiety and tension. Tension might still be lingering in your shoulders, jaw, cheeks, forehead, scalp, or anywhere else in your body. Check everything and notice where you still feel any tension.

Now, visualize a feeling of warmth in those parts. It's a pleasant warmth, not too strong. Visualize that your body is made of chocolate. Your tensed parts are slowly warming up. Then, they begin to melt. It feels so good to melt those parts. They become relaxed, elastic, and soft. There's no stress, tension, or anxiety in those parts anymore.

Enjoy this relaxed feeling, visualizing the smell of warm chocolate. Your body feels like it's being massaged from the inside by your undivided attention.

Now, turn your attention inward again and scan the whole body—notice which part is the most relaxed. Now, visualize this part as a spot of intense, pleasant warmth. This warmth is now spreading through your body in all directions. The zone of warmth grows, spreading relaxation through the whole body. This pleasant warmth fills the whole body until it pushes out even the tiniest pieces of anxiety.

Your whole body is now warm and relaxed. There's nothing else you should be doing right now but enjoying this relaxation and rest. This is your gift to yourself.

Now, focus on your breathing. Our breath is the simplest, yet most powerful thing which keeps us alive. It's also your most powerful cure for anxiety. It can help you calm down, bring your attention to your physical existence, and relax your mind. No thought or fear can survive while you're consciously breathing. Just concentrating on your breathing is enough.

Thoughts will come, for sure, but thoughts will also go. You don't need to fight them. All you need to do is bring your focus back to your breath.

Continue to observe your breathing. Notice everything you can about it. Feel the air entering your nostrils, going down your airways, filling your lungs, and going all the way back out as you exhale. Place your hands on your stomach and feel how your stomach expands as you draw air in. Imagine the emptiness and feel the way of the air leaving your body as you exhale.

Stay with your breath. If you start to feel anxiety, just take another deep breath and focus on the sensation of air filling your lungs.

Breathe in, counting to four—one, two, three, four.

Then, holding your breath, counting to three—one, two, three.

Exhale, counting to eight—one, two, three, four, five, six, seven, eight.

Once again, inhale, counting to four—one, two, three, four.

Holding your breath, count to three—o ne, two, three.

Exhale, counting to eight—one, two, three, four, five, six, seven, eight.

If some thought distracts you, just notice it and let it go. Bring your attention back to your breathing.

Imagine the air you inhale is pure peace and calmness, and the air you exhale is your anxiety. Every time you exhale, you're letting go of tension and anxiety. You're changing it for peace and relaxation.

Feel how the relaxed space becomes bigger and bigger, and the space filled with anxiety shrinks and becomes smaller until it completely disappears. Notice how your breathing soothes and calms you.

Now, while inhaling, mentally say to yourself: "Relax." While you're exhaling, repeat: "Relax."

Once again: inhale—relax, exhale—relax.

Your body is relaxed and your mind is calm. Thoughts are slowing down. You are safe now. Stay calm and feel in control.

Now, in this safe environment, think about how you feel when you are overflowed with anxiety. Tell yourself it's normal to feel that way. The next time you feel that way, remind yourself it's okay and it will pass.

Now, let your mind relax. You don't have to focus on anything anymore. Just rest, relax, and trust everything will be fine.

You are at a special place now. This is the place of inner peace and serenity. There are no worries here. All is well. Not only do you feel relief, but you have also learned how to get to this special place. Just your breath and your focus have brought you here. This is the place within you, and you can get there whenever you want. Here, you can always find shelter and relief from worries and anxiety, even in the middle of the day.

You can stay with this feeling even when you finish with the meditation. This peace can stay with you throughout your usual daily activities.

So the next time you start to feel anxiety, you might simply remember this meditation, and it might be enough to ground you in peace. You'll be able to release anxiety and take back control, breathing deeply, relaxing, and bringing yourself to the present moment.

By practicing this meditation, you'll become more and more confident. You'll know that you are bigger than anything that causes your anxiety.

You are strong. You are calm. You are free. You are peaceful. You are powerful. You are hopeful. You are positive. You are serene.

For those of you who want to go on with your daily activities now that the meditation is over, it's time to wake up. Slowly move your hands and toes, and gently stretch your body. When you feel ready, open your eyes. This peace will stay with you throughout your day.

For those of you who want to fall asleep after the meditation: just go on and enjoy the relaxed feeling that will lull you to sleep. When you wake up, you'll be refreshed and renewed, calm, and relaxed. Sleep well, and have nice dreams.

Guided Meditation for Overcoming Anxiety 2

Welcome to the second guided meditation for relieving anxiety. It has been created to help you change anxiety for balance and inner peace. Through this meditation practice, you'll learn how to detach yourself from disturbing thoughts and emotions, and find serenity.

Before we start, find the most comfortable position and posture. You might want to lie on your back or side, or perhaps you'd like to sit. Whatever you choose, it's okay. Also, don't force yourself to be still—feel free to move during the meditation if you want to. Just follow your gut and make yourself comfortable.

This is time only for you. Everyone needs some time to themselves, to calm their mind and sort through their thoughts. Enjoy this time for rest and recharge—it's a simple, pleasant, yet incredibly powerful cure for anxiety.

Suffering from anxiety often means your mind is hyperactive, crazy busy, and focused on the future. You have rushing thoughts, which make you feel you are in trouble all the time. As if there's always some problem you should be solving or a danger you should run from or fight. These thoughts make you tense and mentally absent. Meanwhile, you pay too little attention to sensations in your body and neglect your breathing. Perhaps your breath is short and shallow, as if you were in real and constant danger.

It would be so nice to have a turn-off button for anxiety, but you can't find it in your mind. Fortunately, there is a button: it is in relaxing your body. When you are tensed, your mind sends signals to the body to prepare for fight or flight. This works in the opposite direction as well. So if you manage to relax your body and calm your breathing, your mind will receive signals to slow down and relax.

Practicing this meditation, you'll learn how to relax your body, deepen your breathing, and slow your mind. That way, your brain will realize you are safe and it will switch off the panic button, stopping your anxiety.

We'll also repeat some mantras to help you remove subconscious blockages and change your beliefs about anxiety.

Now, I invite you to close your eyes and follow my voice. Bring your attention to this very moment.

Become aware of your head and try to contract the tiny muscles of your scalp and forehead. Then relax them. Relax your ears. Feel all the tension in and around your eyes. Then calm that tension , rest, and completely relax. Relax all the muscles of your face. Compress your lips, then let them relax. Clench your jaw, then let it loosen.

Tense the muscles of the back of your neck by pressing the chin against the chest. Then bring your head back and relax your neck.

Contract your shoulder muscles and relax them, letting the shoulders drop down in a relaxed position.

Contract your back muscles, then relax them, feeling how they loosen, one by one, until your whole back is relaxed. Fill your chest with air, and while you exhale, feel the muscles of your chest relaxing.

Pull your navel to your spine, and feel the abdominal muscles tense. Then let your stomach and all those abdominal muscles relax.

Clench your fists, contracting your hands and arms. Then release, relaxing your fingers, palms, wrists, and arms.

Contract your glutes, then slowly relax them. Notice how relaxed the whole body feels when you relax your glutes.

Contract your entire legs, from your hips to thighs, down to your feet and toes. Then relax your hips, relax your thighs, and relax your knees. Relax your ankles, and relax your feet.

Now your whole body is relaxed.

Now, bring awareness to your breathing. You don't have to change anything—just notice how you breathe in and breathe out.

Visualize yourself lying on the grass. It's a beautiful sunny day. There's a clear sky above you. Take a nice, deep breath, and as you're exhaling, imagine you are making soap bubbles. The anxiety from all parts of your body leaves you, filling these bubbles. Then visualize a bubble flying into the sky and popping, releasing your anxiety.

Inhale again, taking all the anxiety you can find, and imagine blowing it into a bubble. Then send it up into the sky. The bubble flies up, up, up, and pops.

Do this once again. Take a breath, letting your stomach expand. Then breathe out all your anxiety, making a lot of bubbles. They fly around you and upward in all directions, taking your anxiety far away. You can see them popping and disappearing.

With your next breath, collect all the anxiety you might still be holding and exhale, making a lot of bubbles. Watch the bubbles fly away.

Now, listen to the affirmations I say and slowly repeat them, mentally or out loud. Dedicate one breath to each of these affirmations.

Inhale, and repeat this mantra as you exhale. *I'm aware of my breathing. I'm aware of the air going in and out of my body.*

Inhale. Exhale, and repeat this mantra. *I'm aware of my body. I'm aware of my heart rhythm.*

Between each of mantra, focus on your inhale and exhale.

I'm aware of my fears and anxiety. I'm aware of the discomfort I feel.

I'm aware of the negative thoughts that make me feel anxious.

Now, as I inhale and exhale, I'm slowly calming my mind.

I'm letting go of negative thoughts.

As I breathe, I'm calming my anxiety.

I'm relaxing my body and slowing down my thoughts.

With each exhale, I'm letting go of fears and concerns.

With each inhale, I'm finding more peace.

I inhale calmness. I exhale peace.

Now, smile while you're breathing.

Being aware of my breathing, I'm letting go of everything that doesn't serve me.

I inhale serenity. I exhale joy.

I am safe and secure. I give myself permission to be in peace.

I am well.

Things are getting better and better every day.

I expect great things to happen.

Now, tell your anxiety: *I see you. It's okay. I accept you and love you.*

I accept all my emotions. I allow myself to experience them. They don't define me. I can observe them while remaining calm.

When you accept your emotions, instead of fighting them, they become lighter. When you set them free, they are able to flow through your body and leave you.

Say to your anxiety, "Thank you for being here to protect me. But I don't need your help anymore. I am ready to let you go now."

Notice how much lighter and freer you feel.

I'm healing all the time. My body and mind are in healthy harmony.

I allow myself to be in peace.

Now, imagine warm, golden light bathing and healing you, part by part, from your head to your toes, wrapping you in a soft glow. It's mighty, yet gentle.

I enjoy being wrapped in a soft, warm blanket. I am safe and secure. It's so good to feel the warm, soft hug of this blanket.

I feel reborn and reenergized now.

I feel wellness in my whole body, in each cell of my body.

I rest in this comfort and peace. I allow myself to slip into tranquility and gentleness.

I enjoy being in this completely relaxed state, free from worries and anxiety.

Now, imagine stairs that lead down. You can picture these stairs however you like. We are going downstairs.

Take a deep breath. Inhale, counting to three—one, two, three.

While exhaling, imagine you are going downstairs, counting your steps to five—one, two, three, four, five.

Inhale, counting to four—one, two, three, four.

Exhale, and move down the stairs, counting to six—one, two, three, four, five, six.

Inhale, counting to five—one, two, three, four, five.

Exhale, counting to seven—one, two, three, four, five, six, seven.

You are in a dark room now. It's not completely dark here, but you can barely see where you're going. Don't be afraid. You are safe.

Take a few steps into the room. You are in the center of the room. Imagine sitting on the floor with your legs crossed. Although it's dark in here, you can see there is an item on the floor, in front of you. It's a bowl.

You pick up the bowl and hold it in your hands. It's heavy. Its surface is smooth and cold. You can't clearly see its color, but you know it's dark.

Now, put it back on its place on the floor in front of you.

Picture your anxiety as dark sand collected in your body.

Imagine taking your anxiety, as much of it as you can grab with your hands. Put it in the bowl. Repeat this a few times.

Imagine your worries and concerns as dark, cold stones in your mind. Take them and put them into the bowl.

Repeat this action with each worry that bothers you, causing your anxiety.

Now, you've put all your anxiety, worries, and negative thoughts into the bowl.

Breathe deeply, filling your belly.

Everything is constantly changing.

Dark can turn into light.

Your worries and anxiety can change into acceptance, peace, love, power, and joy.

Notice that the bowl becomes lighter. You can clearly see the bowl now. It becomes lighter with each of your breaths. Dark sand becomes lighter too. Then, the sand starts to glow in the dark. It's a shiny powder, like glitter. The dark stones you have put into the bowl also become lighter and lighter. Now they shine brightly, like jewels. The bowl shines with bright, golden light, spreading this light all over the room. You are sitting in the bright, clean light, inhaling it.

Your thoughts have changed from dark and heavy to glimmering jewels full of luck and wonderful possibilities. As you inhale, the whole body fills with bright, healing light. Now you glow. You are peace. You are love. You are light.

When a dark thought comes to you again, you can direct it into this bowl. The bowl will turn this dark thought into light. This bowl will always be here for you.

You can come back here whenever you wish.

When you are ready, you can slowly stand up and go back to the stairs. You can take the light and your bright jewels full of positive thoughts with you.

We are going upstairs. Take a deep breath and count backward with me—six, five, four, three, two, one.

You are back in your usual surroundings. But there is one significant change—you are calm and peaceful. You are spreading the light, and you know you can come back to take more of this light whenever you need.

When you feel ready, take a deep breath. Exhale, and gently open your eyes. You can go on with your activities, feeling much lighter and calmer than before.

Guided Meditation for Panic Attack Relief

Welcome to the guided meditation for panic relief.

If you are having a panic attack right now, it's great you're here.

A panic attack can be very frightening, especially if you go through it alone, without anyone by your side. This meditation is here to support you while you're experiencing these unpleasant moments and help you get back to a state of calm.

These uneasy feelings and sensations you are having will soon pass. You might feel out of control or disconnected from your surroundings, or that something terrible will happen. You may feel that you're losing your mind or you're going to die.

But rest assured, although those sensations are very unpleasant, they will all pass. You will be okay. You are okay even now.

What you are going through is normal, although it doesn't seem so. It's a natural neurological response and cannot last for an extended period of time. It's not physically possible, because the hormones that make you feel so diminish. So this feeling will fade away.

You may already know all this, but when you're experiencing a panic attack, your survival instinct might override your rational mind. It's hard not to believe the irrational, frightening thoughts that you're having. These thoughts are all part of a fight or flight mode, and that's how our bodies and minds work. It's part of human nature—that's why it can be so hard to calm down. That's why you need reassurance that you are okay and a reminder that this will all pass. All those uncomfortable, scary, unbearable feelings you're having right now will pass.

Maybe you are also experiencing physical symptoms. Maybe you can't breathe properly, catch your breath, or maybe your heart is racing and you feel dizziness, numbness, or tingling...These sensations are all normal, and they will pass.

Let's do some calm breathing together, which will help you calm down.

Even if you feel like you can't breathe properly, you are able to breathe. It's just your mind playing tricks on you.

Say something out loud—anything. Remember, if you can talk, you can breathe.

You're probably forgetting to exhale. And that is normal when you feel endangered.

Now, visualize a lot of candles in front of you. Like on a birthday cake, for example.

Now, take a breath in, and blow out a candle.

Breathe in, slowly, through your nose. Hold it. Now, breathe out, slowly, through your mouth.

Once again--breathe in. Hold. Breathe out.

In. Hold. Out.

Everything is okay. You have enough air.

If you want, you can go on with breathing this way. Or, if you like, look around at your surroundings.

Notice everything you see.

Notice all the sounds around you.

Your anxious feelings will pass because they are not based on anything real. Your mind is playing tricks on you. You are safe, and everything is okay.

Sometimes, it can help a lot during a panic attack to drink a cold glass of water. Or, if it's nighttime, you can turn off the lights. It can also help to wash your face with cool water.

Looking through a window, counting all trees or roofs in sight can also help you distract yourself from these unpleasant bodily sensations.

Maybe none of these actions will help you right now. And that's okay, because even if you do absolutely nothing, this feeling will pass.

You don't have to do anything at all. You don't have to think, focus, or talk. We can just wait together for this feeling to fade away. Just listen to my voice, if it helps.

This unpleasant feeling will get smaller and smaller until it disappears, I promise. You will be calm again.

Now, look around and notice your surroundings. Notice the colors, the light, and the textures of your surroundings. Listen to the sounds you hear. Notice your body's weight against the surface below you, or the feeling of your feet against the surface.

You are okay, even though you don't feel okay right now.

Maybe you feel a bit disconnected from your body right now. Let's do a grounding technique that will help you feel connected with your body again.

To start, squeeze your hands into fists, and tighten the muscles of your arms. Feel the tension building in your shoulders, arms, and hands. Hold them tensed for a moment. Then, let them loosen. Feel the weight of your arms as they relax. Allow your shoulders to drop.

Take a deep breath in, hold it in, and breathe out through your mouth.

Let's squeeze these body parts again, but this time, include your face. Squeeze your hands, arms, and shoulders, and crunch up all your face muscles. Squeeze them tighter and tighter. Hold for a moment. Now relax.

Let your shoulders soften, and let your arms and hands relax. Allow your face to relax.

Rub your hands together, then gently place them over your eyes. Feel the warmth radiating from your palms. Notice the sensation of warm palms over your cheeks.

Now, bring your hands back into their relaxed position.

Breathe in. Hold it in. Breathe out deeply, as if you're blowing candles.

Maybe you notice your anxiety starting to fade. If not, that's okay. Sometimes, it requires more time.

Simply accepting a panic attack and anxiety for what they are and not trying to eliminate them will help. Notice how you feel. It doesn't matter if you good or bad—just notice. Let go of all resistance.

Try to soften your body as much as you can. Are there areas that are extra-tensed—your throat, neck, jaw, or anywhere else? Try to soften them intentionally, even if it's just a little.

Everything changes, always. This unpleasant feeling will change too. You just need to let that chnage happen. Feeling anxious is not bad. It is what it is, a physical reaction. Nothing different from the flu or any body ache. It's okay. Anxiety may be scary, but it can't hurt you.

Breathe in. Hold. Breathe out.

You are safe. Everything's okay.

Now, allow yourself to rest and allow your relaxation response to kick in.

While you do that, listen to these affirmations. Eventually, you'll begin to feel even calmer.

Take a deep breath in through your nose. Breathe out through your mouth.

Go on with breathing like this, deeply and slowly.

I accept the way I feel right now.

It's okay to be anxious.

This anxiety will soon fade.

I accept how I feel at this moment.

I know this feeling will soon pass.

I accept whatever I am feeling.

I will not resist.

I'm feeling calmer and more relaxed.

I will be okay.

I am okay.

I am safe.

I already feel a bit calmer and more relaxed than a moment ago.

I am feeling so much more relaxed.

I am breathing much easier now.

My muscles are more relaxed.

My face is smooth and relaxed.

My throat feels open and relaxed.

My chest feels lighter.

My heart is calmer.

My belly is soft.

I am calm.

I am at ease.

My thoughts are slowing down.

With each passing moment, I feel better and better.

I know I am safe.

I am peaceful.

I am relaxed.

I am calm.

I am serene.

I am at ease.

I am peaceful, relaxed, calm, and at ease.

I am safe, and all is well.

Guided Meditation for Overcoming Depression

Welcome to this meditation designed to help you with depression and depressive moods.

During this meditation session, you'll gain a new perspective and learn a new way to look at your thoughts and feelings.

As soon as you finish this meditation, you may find you'll feel better. You'll immediately feel more hopeful.

If you regularly practice this meditation, you'll feel depressed less often. Eventually, you'll notice depression has disappeared from your life and you have your old self back again.

Yet, keep in mind that this meditation is meant to ease depression and help you during the process, but it can't replace professional help. So please, seek professional help and use this meditation as a supplement.

To begin, choose a time when you won't be disturbed and you're free to safely close your eyes, listen, and relax for a while. Remember, this quiet, "me time" is not a luxury. It's a need and will tremendously enrich your healing.

Before we begin with the meditation, take time to find a comfortable position. You can be lying or sitting. It's up to you, and everything is okay as long as your back is straight yet relaxed.

Make sure your clothes feel comfortable, and loosen all restrictive belts or pieces. Turn off any ringers and notifications.

Place your hands beside your body. Or, place them on your lap or knees, with your palms turned up.

If you wish, close your eyes. If you want to keep them open, that's okay, too.

Take a few deep and slow breaths. Connect with your breath. Observe how it affects your body. Notice all the sensations and movements connected with it. Feel the air entering your nostrils. Notice your belly rising and falling with the in-breaths and the out-breaths.

Now, allow your breathing to settle into its natural rhythm and let go of trying to control it.

Be aware of your body, its posture, its place in the space around you, and its weight on the surface beneath you.

Notice all sensations in the body. Feel all your body parts.

Remain aware of your breathing and its natural rhythm.

Depression is universal. It's part of being human. We all feel depressed from time to time. But when it lasts for a long time, it affects everything—our bodies and our health, along with our mindset, thinking, emotions, and all aspects of life. There's a whole package of negative feelings coming from depression. It can make you look at life through dark glasses, leaving you unable to see anything positive. Eventually, it seems as if all your interests have faded away.

Depression is a natural reaction to loss. However, you can also be depressed for no apparent reason. That doesn't make your depression any easier, nor does it mean anything is wrong with you. Either way, know that your thoughts and emotions are normal.

Although depression is tough and not at all fun, depression can bring you something good. It can compel you to turn inward, examine your problems and perspectives, gain meaningful insights, reevaluate things in your life, and make adjustments to your life.

Certainly, living with depression is not something you should accept as permanent. Know there is always a solution out there for it. Seek professional help and support from people around you. Use this meditation as often as you can. This meditation will teach you techniques that will help you feel better. You can use these techniques whenever you need them.

Whatever your emotions and thoughts are, you should not ignore, suppress, or deny them. Whatever you fight or deny grows stronger. So the solution is not in digging for the root of the problem and figuring out where it comes from. This is not the ways to get rid of negative thoughts and feelings. A better solution is to change your relationship with them.

Instead of resisting and fighting hard feelings, accept them, make space for them to play, and stay with them for a while. Give them your attention—your emotions are trying to tell you something. They are telling you where you are not faithful to your true self.

So when you offer your emotions acceptance instead of resistance, you'll see, much to your surprise, how they lose their power and fade away.

Now, make yourself comfortable so you can relax. If you fall asleep during the meditation, that's okay—your subconscious mind will be listening to and recording everything I say. But, if possible, try to stay alert during the session so you can consciously engage in your healing.

Breathe in and out your natural pattern. You don't need to change your rhythm or depth of breathing for now. Just breathe in your usual way.

Place your attention on your nose. Feel the air entering your nostrils. Feel the coolness of the air. Now, notice the air leaving your nostrils. Notice its warmth.

Do this for a few moments. Focus on breathing cool air in and warm air out. Concentrate only on the sensations in your nose.

Do it once again—cool air in, warm air out.

Now, explore your breath and allow yourself to experience it fully. Watch your breath and be curious. Feel the experience of breathing, and observe yourself having that experiecnce at the same time.

If your natural breathing is long and deep, notice that. If your normal breathing is short and shallow, notice that, too, without judgment. If your breathing changes or stays the same, notice that. Don't try to change or fix anything. Don't think about "how things should be." Instead, accept things for what they are and just observe them without trying to control them.

For now, we are still observing your natural breathing pattern.

Sooner or later, you will lose your focus. That is perfectly normal, so don't criticize or judge yourself. We all get distracted, and focusing requires some practice.

Distractions always come from one of these sources: your thoughts, sensations, or feelings. When a distraction occurs, just notice it and let it go. Then, gently bring your focus back to your breath. Try to do it for a moment, until the next distraction. When you're distracted again, notice, and let it go. No need to push it away. Don't fight it, don't suppress it. Just let it float by.

Whenever your mind begins to wander, notice that too. Bring your attention back to your nose and the sensations in it as you breathe in and out.

It's also expected to feel the urge to name a distraction. For instance, you may mentally say to yourself, "The alarm is ringing in the next apartment", "kids are making noise outside", "there is traffic", "the dog's barking," or name whatever is distracting you.

Try to name just one thing instead, more general and more in connection with what's happening inside you— you can see "distraction" or "wandering", for instance. Always bring your attention back to your breathing. Try this for a moment, with the next distraction or when your mind wanders again.

Now, the next time you lose your focus, try not to name things at all—even mentally. Just notice that you have lost your focus and bring it back. Try doing this with the next distraction.

Most likely, depressed thoughts and feelings will intrude. These are the ones you are trying to escape from. The trick is to always bring your attention back to your breathing instead of following those thoughts.

Just breathe in your natural way. When a negative thought arises, just notice it and let it pass by. this will get easier each time because you already know how to let thoughts go by gently bringing your focus back to your nose and your breathing.

So try this for a moment. Notice the negative thought occurring. Let it float by you, easily, without your trying to push it away.

When you feel depressed, your mind is often stuck in the past, ruminating about some things from the past that have affected your life. Being in the present, and being consciously aware, makes you balanced. You are the most present when focusing on your breath and the sensations in your body. This focus makes you fully grounded in the present.

Try to be consciously present and aware of each moment of your next few breaths. Feel the air entering your nostrils. Feel its coolness. Feel it as it goes down your airways to your lungs and belly. Notice all the movements connected with your breath. Feel all the sensation it provokes in your body. Follow its way back, and feel the warmth of the air leaving your nostrils.

Doing this, be intentionally present and completely aware of every moment of your next few breaths.

Don't be surprised when negative emotions occur and distract you. These emotions go hand in hand with depressive thoughts. You'll probably feel emotions of sadness, emptiness, anxiety, resentment, bitterness, anger, or rage.

Emotions are nothing but a combination of your thoughts and your physical sensations. Acknowledge that fact, and mentally divide a negative emotion into those two parts. Notice the thought in your mind and feel the sensation it provokes in your body. You might feel the sensation as tension in your head or neck, weight on your chest, or fatigue, monotony, or an ache in various body parts. Allow yourself to experience what you feel. You don't need to change it, solve it, or take any action about it.

The second part is to see the thoughts in your mind. Acknowledge the connection between your thoughts and your physical sensations. Your thoughts provoke bodily sensations, and you experience those two together as an emotion.

Make a conscious choice to place your attention on a sensation in your body, not the thought. Rest your attention on the sensation. Notice if its intensity changes or stays the same. The sensation might even disappear under your focused attention.

Now, leave the emotion and the sensation in your body, and gently bring your attention back to your breathing and the way it feels in your nose. Breathe in, and feel the cool air entering your nose. Breathe out, and focus on the warmth of the air that's leaving your nose.

If you choose to follow your distressing thoughts, it will strengthen your connected negative sensations. But if you choose to pay undivided attention to your negative sensations, your depressing and distressing thoughts diminish. These sensations need your negative thoughts and their stories to feed themselves. So if you focus only on your physical sensations, negative emotions starve and fade away, bringing you relief.

Notice that focusing on your breathing and physical sensation grounds you in the present and brings you relief better than anything else.

Now, visualize that you are at a train station. People are rushing in all directions. There is hustle and bustle all around you. You are standing still on your platform, waiting for your train. The world around you seems dull and grey—colorless people wearing gray suits, dirty streets around the station, a gray station, and ugly trains. You are wearing a plain, gray robe with no defined shape. You are also carrying a heavy bag made of dark leather. It's so heavy that your arms are sore. But you can't put it down. You have to carry it wherever you go.

Thoughts may come and go in their rhythm while you observe the world around you. Don't worry, all the mental chatter will pass. Just let the thoughts be, and be gentle with yourself. Both people and your thoughts are passing by you in their busy manner, but you remain completely calm. You know you will be leaving this hectic environment in a moment, as soon as your train arrives.

Think of this moment as an escape that will help you think clearly again. The train will take you to a far destination, where you will feel peaceful and calm. You know you'll come back to this station as a different person. You are ready to begin the journey.

Your train arrives, and you are stepping aboard. Give yourself permission to devote this time to yourself, spend some time alone, and relax. You know you'll gain a new perspective, and you also know that this has to be done. So don't feel guilty.

You find your carriage. It's empty, and you are the only passenger here. Take a seat and finally put your heavy bag down. It's such a relief to finally put it down! Your muscles automatically relax. A sense of tranquility fills your mind and body.

Voices from the station start to fade away. You are looking through a window. It's the same dull and grey world out there, but you can observe it from a distance now. You are leaving it behind now, and it's natural to feel sadness, regret, or relief, knowing that you are leaving everything that was holding you back.

Take this your time to rest and relax. Allow yourself to see your needs and desires. Your sadness is trying to tell you something. Perhaps it's trying to show you that you have neglected your needs and needs of your soul. So your body suffers and processes unpleasant feelings to gain your attention. You have enough time now to relax the whole body.

You've created a distance now, and you can see your life from another perspective. From your window, the world outside looks different now. The sky looks bluer and clearer, and the grass and trees are greener.

The farther you get from the train station, the easier you feel. Your feel calm and positive. Your arms and hands are resting from carrying your heavy bag. Your muscles are relaxed in a comfortable seat. Your breathing is deep and slow. Your stomach is quiet and steady. Your legs and feet are comfortable and relaxed. Your mind slows down to a pleasant speed. You feel free to just be yourself, in balance, and let everything just be as it is.

As the train reaches your destination, it stops. You pick up your heavy, black bag and step off the train. You have just a few more streets to walk to your special place.

The bag is too heavy, but you know you won't have to carry it for much longer. You feel stronger now, as well as determined and enthusiastic.

You come to a stop in front of a large gate. You open it. You are in your private garden.

It's been a long time since you were here last time. The garden looks neglected. No one was taking care of it while you were occupied with your sadness and pain.

You step on the path that leads through the garden. There are no flowers or grass. Instead, there are weeds.

You go to an old tree at the back of the garden. There's a spade leaning against a tree. You take it and starting to dig. You dig a hole in the shade of the tree. Once you're done digging, you open the bag, curious to find out what was the heavy load you were carrying around.

To your surprise, the bag is full of your worries, fears, sadness, anger, and regrets. You can see them all as large, heavy stones. It's time to bury them now.

Now, take the rocks, one by one, and drop them into the hole you've dug. Name your stones by your unpleasant feelings and mentally say to each of them while dropping it into the hole, "I'm letting you go."

Let go of sadness.

Let go of regrets.

Let go of anger.

Let go of self-doubt.

Let go of resentment.

Let go of bitterness.

Let go of monotony.

Let go of hatred.

Let go of jealousy.

Let go of misery.

Let go of helplessness.

Let go of hopelessness.

Let go of fears.

Let go of the pain.

Let go of suffering.

Let go of everything that makes you feel bad.

Do this as long as you need to bury all the stones from your bag. In the end, bury the bag too. Recover the hole with dirt, and feel the relief.

Now, go back to an old bench in the middle of the garden. Take a seat on the bench and enjoy the feeling of ease and freedom. Feel the lightness. Notice the sun shining through the trees. Look around.

Nurturing this garden needs just a little energy to fix everything and bring back its old glow. Taking care of this place is your priority now. You know you'll enjoy every moment of it and the results of tending to it.

Rest deeply in your garden, imaging its final look once you've taken care of everything. Inhale the sunlight. Exhale peace. Look at the colorful flowers. Smell the roses. Feel your enthusiasm. Realize that your journey brought you here to remind you of who you really are. Your old self is back now.

Smile at who you really are. Enjoy watching the dance of light and shadows in your garden, and mentally say to yourself:

I am free.

I am relaxed.

I am peaceful.

I am grateful.

I am light.

I am happy.

I am energetic.

I am full of love.

I am calm.

I am safe.

I am powerful.

I am joyful.

Life is good.

Life is colorful.

Life is magnificent.

I love myself.

I know my value.

I appreciate myself.

I accept myself.

I love life.

I am free.

I am relaxed.

I am peaceful.

I am grateful.

I am light.

I am happy.

I am energetic.

I am full of love.

I am calm.

I am safe.

I am powerful.

I am joyful.

Life is good.

Life is colorful.

Life is magnificent.

I love myself.

I know my value.

I appreciate myself.

I accept myself.

I love life.

Breathe deeply, and smile to yourself with every exhale.

Enjoy being in this relaxed state for a while, feeling the warm sunlight on your skin. You can take this feeling with you wherever you go.

When you come back from this trip to your usual life, you will have a completely different perspective.

Your private garden will always be there for you. You can come back to it whenever you wish.

When you feel ready, gently open your eyes and go on with your usual daily activities. Or, you can drift off to sleep and have a deep rest.

Guided Meditation for Overcoming Insomnia

Good evening. Welcome to this guided meditation that will help you overcome insomnia.

If you have problems with falling asleep or staying asleep during the night, this meditation is for you. You can use it whether you frequently have trouble sleeping, or just from time to time.

It's not pleasant at all to lie sleeplessly in your bed and feel exhausted the next day, unable to give a quality rest to your body and mind.

Use this meditation before sleep as part of your evening routine.

Prepare yourself for bed in your usual way. Lie down on your bed and find the most comfortable position. The temperature should also be pleasant—not too warm, not too cold. You can lie on your back or on your side—whatever position best helps you relax.

I invite you to listen to my voice. Let my voice guide you, help you relax, and take you to a calm, calm state from which you can easily fall asleep.

My words in this meditation will speak to your both conscious and subconscious mind. That way, I will help you easily fall asleep and stay asleep for the whole night.

Finally, you'll have a restful sleep that will recharge you. The sleep you'll enjoy will be the first time in a long time that you won't wake up during the night. You'll finally feel rested and refreshed in the morning.

However, this might not happen the first few times you do this meditation. But what will undoubtedly happen is that you will relax more and feel less tensed.

A good night's sleep is a habit. To build a habit of easily falling asleep and staying asleep throughout the night, you will need time and practice. But once you've established this habit, it will pay off in levels of energy and life satisfaction. So it's worth a try.

I recommend that you be patient and consistent in using this meditation every night before sleep. It will undoubtedly lead to forming better sleep habits, and eventually overcoming insomnia. The first time you fall asleep and stay asleep until the morning, waking up renewed and refreshed, you'll realize that all your efforts have paid off and this was the best thing you could do for yourself.

We often have a hard time trying to relax and fall asleep because our minds refuse to stop thinking. When our body tries to calm down to sleep, our brain seems to find it the best time to go into overdrive.

If you are one of many people who overthink, especially when it's time for sleep, you can't stop thinking. It would be best to write all your thoughts down. That way, you'll put these thoughts aside for later, without any worry that you might forget something important. You'll also free up space in your mind, allowing it to calm down.

So, pause this meditation and transfer all your pressing thoughts from your mind to a piece of paper. Your concerns and actions can wait. Now, it is time for rest.

I now invite you to put your attention on my voice and ground yourself in this very moment. Feel the comfort and the warmth of your bed. Feel the ease, because it is a time when you don't need to do anything. This is time only for you and your reenergizing.

You don't have to do a thing. Just listen to my voice without any expectation, especially an expectation of falling asleep. Even if you stay awake all night long, this meditation will still bring you relaxation and rest. So don't put any pressure on yourself. All you need to do is lie in your bed, listen to my words, and relax. If sleep comes, great. If not, no big deal. You will still get rest.

Take a deep breath in, to the count of four. Hold the breath to the count of three. Breathe out as slowly as you can, counting to six.

Repeat this sequence a few more times. Take a deep breath in, to the count of four. Hold the breath to the count of three. Breathe out as slowly as you can, counting to six.

Do it once again Inhale—one, two, three, four. Hold it—one, two, three. Exhale—one, two, three, four, five, six.

And one more time, breathe in deeply, counting to four. Hold the breath the count of three. Then breathe out, counting to six.

If you can't reach these numbers, that's okay. Don't force yourself—just do what you can.

Then, allow your breathing to fall back into its usual rhythm.

With each breath out, allow your body to relax a bit more and sink deeper into the surface beneath you.

Now, watch your thoughts come and go. They come and go all the time. Your busy mind is used to producing them all the time. But you don't have to follow each and every one of them.

This insight is a precious one—you are not your thoughts. Even more so, you can always choose which of your thoughts you want to think about. Your thoughts are just products of your mind, and you are the one who decides which ones to think about.

So if you're going to rest your busy mind and fall asleep, let your thoughts float by like little clouds or soap bubbles. Since you can't forbid your mind to do its job and create thoughts, the only thing you can do is to remove your focus from your thoughts. Focus on something else, and unwanted thoughts will lose their power and diminish. Eventually, your mind will slow down and stop creating them. That's why mindful focus on your breathing, physical sensations, and environment can go a long way to relax and calm a busy mind.

Now, bring your awareness to your body and its sensations. This is always the first step towards mindful presence.

Notice how your body feels. Acknowledge its posture, and feel the temperature of your body and the space around it. Feel the support of the surface beneath you and the comfort of your mattress. Feel the weight of your body and the weights of bed covers on top of you. Feel your heartbeat and the rhythm of your blood flow. Focus on your breathing and listen to its sounds.

Place your attention on your nose. Feel the air entering your nostrils and going down to fill your lungs. Note how you fill your stomach with the air and allow your stomach to inflate like a balloon. Then, follow the way of the breath back, noticing how it leaves your stomach, your lungs, and finally, your nostrils. Notice the coolness of the air you are inhaling, and the warmth of it when you exhale it after it went through your body.

Continue to focus only on your breathing and movement, along with the sensations it provokes in your body. This process is the easiest and quickest way to ground yourself and relax.

How do your feet feel? How do your legs feel? Notice sensations in each part of the body. How do your glutes and pelvic area feel? What do you feel in your stomach? How does your back feel? Notice all the sensations in your fingers, hands, and arms. Acknowledge how your shoulders and neck feel. Then, bring your awareness to sensations in your head and face.

If there is any tension in your body, acknowledge it. Allow all the tension to rise from the deep or hidden corners of your body, coming up to the surface. When you feel that all the tension is collecting on your skin, let it go.

Take a deep breath, and with your exhale, let go of tension.

Repeat this process a few times until you feel your body is completely relaxed, free from any tension.

Do another quick scan of the whole body, part by part, checking if all the parts are relaxed.

If you find any tension, simply let it go with breathing out.

There are so many things you can place your focus on right now. Even the busiest mind calms when you are mindful and truly present.

Sooner or later, your focus will drift off from your breathing and physical sensations. Gently bring your focus back. Concentrating on the feelings in your body and on your breathing is the simplest, yet most powerful way to stay present, grounded, calm, and relaxed.

Thoughts will eventually appear in your mind. Don't stress about that happening. Notice your thoughts, and let them go. Do this as many times as needed, always bringing your focus back to your breath and your body. Notice the air entering your nose, and stay with the breath throughout the body, moment by moment. This is a natural way to calm yourself and, after some time, drift off to sleep.

So breathe in, breathe out, and, with a smile, greet the wonderful feeling of relaxation and letting go. This is time only for you. This is time to recharge and gain fresh energy.

Stretch your body and feel how comfortable it is to lie in your bed, having nothing else to do. The night is meant for having rest from everyone and everything, including our thoughts. So with every breath, dive deeper into the sense of comfort and relaxation.

Now, visualize that you are on a canoe on calm, clear water. The canoe is floating on the water, cradling you gently. Listen to the lapping sounds of the water. Your eyes are closed, and the sun is shining tenderly on your skin. Your boat is incredibly comfortable, as soft as a cloud, yet strong enough to support you. You are safe and calm.

Feel the joy and the ease of this moment. It's beautiful. Breathe in, breathe out, and smile to yourself.

The canoe is large enough for your whole body to lie down comfortably. It's time for you to relax the whole body, part by part, by scanning it with your mindful attention, healing light, and your inner smile.

Begin by relaxing your toes and feet. Allow them to gently open to the ceiling. Relax all the muscles of your legs. Relax your lower and upper legs. Relax your knees. Relax your hips and pelvic area. Relax your glutes, and notice how now the whole lower part of your body is relaxed. Allow your fingers to relax, and open your palms to the ceiling. Relax your wrists, and all of your hands and arms.

Place your inner smile into your belly. Feel the calmness and peace in your stomach. Allow it to move easily in the rhythm of your breathing. Notice how relaxed it is. Relax your chest, and feel it floating.

Now, relax your back from the lowest point up to your neck. Relax your vertebrae, one by one, and feel each muscle loosening and relaxing. Your back becomes soft, as during a massage. Breathe in and breathe out, visualizing that you are exhaling through your spine everything you want to let go.

Our shoulders are the most crucial area in relaxation. They are where we hold and carry most of the weight, such as our worries, fears, and uncomfortable feelings. Most of us go through life not noticing that our shoulders are tensed and tight. So relax your shoulders now. Let go of all the weight, and let your shoulders drop from your ears.

Relax your neck, allowing it to loosen and soften, leaving your head cradled by the soft pillow. Open up your throat and allow all the muscles in there to relax.

The muscles of the head are often tensed and overwhelmed. Let all these muscles relax. Relax your scalp and your forehead. Relax your eyebrows, and all the tiny muscles around your eyes. Allow your eyes to rest into the head. They work hard all day long, so it's time for them to finally have a proper rest.

Relax your cheeks and your lips. Release your jaw and allow the base of your tongue to relax. Relax your ears.

Intentionally release any other tension you might be still feeling in your head and face.

Once again, do another quick scan of the whole body to check that it is completely relaxed.

Your feet—relaxed. Your legs, knees, upper legs—relaxed. Your hips and pelvis—relaxed. Your glutes—relaxed. Your hands—relaxed. Your arms, elbows, and upper arms—relaxed. Your belly—relaxed. Your chest—

relaxed. Your back, from the bottom to the top—relaxed. Your shoulders and neck—relaxed. The top of your bead and the back of your head—relaxed. Your face—relaxed. Your eye muscles, your nose, your cheeks, your mouth, your jaw—all relaxed.

Now, when all the parts of your body are relaxed, it's time to pay attention to your skin and allow it to relax too. Your skin works all the time, protecting your body from the outside world. It also needs rest and reenergizing.

Now, visualize the other organs in your body. Take a moment to appreciate everything they do for you all the time. Smile at them with your inner smile, send them love and light, and allow them to relax. Imagine your body on the inside. Imagine your organs working for you all the time. Mentally send them love, and let them relax.

Acknowledge that your emotional parts also need rest. Emotions are turned on all the time, but you don't need them to be on right now. Give your emotions permission to let go. Forgive everything there is to be forgiven. Let go of all negative feelings. The only thing you need now is inner peace and tranquility. Don't hold any anger, resentment, nor sadness. Let go of everything that doesn't serve you.

If any thoughts occur, and they certainly will, let them pass you by. You don't need any of them right now. It is not time to think about or solve problems, be productive, or achieve anything. It is time to rest your mind. Let your mind rest and recharge now so you can be productive when the time for that comes.

Now, visualize you are in a dark, empty room. The only thing you can see is a clock on the wall. The clock hands are moving at the speed of your thoughts. The only thing you should do is count the movements of the clock hands.

You find counting the hands' movements harder and harder, because they move slower and slower. You are becoming more and more sleepy. You notice the hands' movements become slower and slower until they are barely moving at all.

Your mind is calm and clear now. You are just a step away from drifting off to sleep.

Observe your body becoming heavier and sleepier. You are in a state of deep relaxation now. Watch your slow and deep breathing, your calm mind, and your relaxed body. There's no need to change anything. There's only calm, mindful observation and acceptance. You feel the warmth, coziness, peace, and deep calmness. Everything's calm, peaceful, and easy. Everything you don't need fades away into the blurry background. Inhale. Exhale.

This is how it feels to be relaxed on a deep level.

You are carefree. All is well. Breathe in, breathe out.

Let go of all your concerns, fears, and worries. Everything will be just fine. Everything happens when the time is perfect. Leave everything to higher intelligence, and trust all will be well.

Enjoy the serenity and carefreeness of giving up control, and allow a dream to come.

This is a moment of perfect balance and harmony.

Notice your deep, calm breathing. Feel the comfort and ease of becoming one with the moment, releasing any effort. Your body and mind are enjoying these moments of absolute rest.

You are now in a forest, high in the mountains. The sun is shining through the trees. You've been hiking in the forest all day long. You feel pretty tired now, but your house is still quite far away. So you have to walk about an hour more until you get there. You know that a fire in the fireplace, a cozy blanket, and a warm, comfortable bed are waiting for you.

You're stepping down a steep, narrow path. You feel so tired that you start to count your steps to move your attention from your sore feet. You are walking and breathing in the fresh mountain air, counting your breaths one by one. Breathe in, breathe out—one. Breathe in, breathe out—two. Breathe in, breathe out—three. Breathe in, breathe out—four. Breathe in, breathe out—five.

Your feet are tired. Your legs are sleepy. Your back needs rest. Your mind is sluggish. Your eyes are struggling to stay open. Your hands are limp. You are yawning, wishing only one thing—to get to your house soon and sink into bed.

You're going down the steep path. You know you have to get home before the day ends. You can hear birds and insects in the grass, your steps down the path, and the sound of your breathing.

You are still breathing deeply, counting each inhale and exhale. The night is about to come. The forest is preparing for sleep. It becomes harder and harder to walk and count as you become more and more sleepy. You wish to lie under the tree and just let yourself fall asleep.

You are yawning and can barely walk. Fortunately, just a few more steps, and you'll get to the small house where you can finally sleep. The moon and stars appear in the sky.

You finally reach your destination. You open the wooden door. Your legs are heavy, and you can barely move. A warm fire is crackling in the fireplace.

You lie down on your cozy bed, placing your head onto a soft, fluffy pillow, wrapping yourself in a warm blanket.

You can feel your legs are already sleeping. Your stomach is sleeping. Your back is sleeping. Your head is sleeping. Your face is sleeping. Your whole body is sleeping. It's now time to allow your mind to fall asleep too.

Mentally repeat those statements:

I am calm.

I am peaceful.

I am tranquil.

I am free.

I am worth everything life has to give me.

I am full of love.

I am healing.

I am recharging.

I am reenergizing.

I am resting.

I am divinely supported and guided.

I am safe.

I am secure.

I feel good.

I feel comfortable.

I feel light.

I feel serene.

Everything's all right.

I'm free to rest now.

While you fall asleep, acknowledge that all is well. You'll have a good, quality rest tonight. You'll fall asleep now, and stay asleep throughout the whole night. In the morning, you'll wake up refreshed and renewed.

Feel the serenity. Feel the calmness. Feel the tranquility and deep peace. Allow yourself to sink into a deeper sleep, knowing everything is fine. You are calm. You are safe. You are worthy. You deserve good rest.

Step into the sleeping state, where all the problems of the day are solved.

Good night, and have a nice sleep.

www.ingramcontent.com/pod-product-compliance
Lightning Source LLC
Chambersburg PA
CBHW070043120526
44589CB00035B/2300